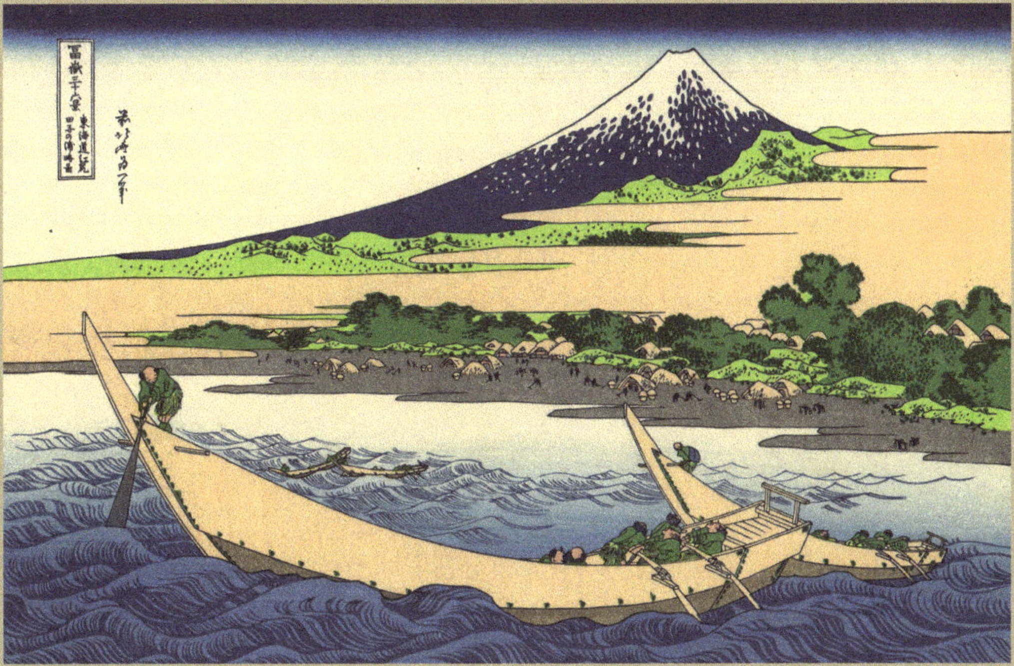

Thirty-Six Views of Mount Fuji

Thirty-Six Views of Mount Fuji

haibun by

Martin Willitts Jr.

woodblock prints by

Katsushika Hokusai

(1760–1849)

SHANTI ARTS PUBLISHING

BRUNSWICK, MAINE

Thirty-Six Views of Mount Fuji

Published by Shanti Arts Publishing

Designed by Shanti Arts Designs

Shanti Arts LLC
193 Hillside Road
Brunswick, Maine 04011

shantiarts.com

Printed in the United States of America

ISBN: 978-1-962082-14-3 (softcover)

Library of Congress Control Number: 2024933126

Contents

Acknowledgments:

Broadkill River Review: "South Wind, Clear Sky (Red Fuji)" and "Sundai in Edo"

Ekphrastic Review: "The Great Wave off Kanagawa"; "Tama River in Musashi Province"; "Umezawa in Sagami Province"; and "Watermill at Ondenv"

Foreign Literary Journal: "Mount Fuji Reflects in Lake Kawaguchi, Seen from the Misaka Pass in Kai Province"; "Senju, Musashi Province"; "A Sketch of the Mitsui Shop in Suruga in Edo"

Muddy River Poetry Review: "The Lake of Hakone in Sagami Province"

Naugatuck River Review: "Sunset across the Ryōgoku Bridge from the Bank of the Sumida River at Onmayagashi"

Skin Deep Anthology (Glass Lyre Press): "The Kazusa Province Sea Route"

Switchgrass Review: "Mount Fuji from the Mountains of Tōtōmi"

Transpacificism: "Asakusa Hongan-ji Temple in the Eastern Capital"; "Barrier Town on the Sumida River"; "Bay of Noboto"; "Below Meguro"; "Cushion Pine at Aoyama"; "Enoshima in Sagami Province"; "Fuji View Field in Owari Province"; "Hodogaya on the Tōkaidō"; "Inume Pass, Kōshū"; "Kajikazawa in Kai Province"; "Lake Suwa in Shinano Province"; "Mishima Pass in Kai Province"; "Mount Fuji from the Mountains of Tōtōmi"; "Rainstorm Beneath the Summit"; "Sazai Hall—Temple of Five Hundred Rakan"; and "Shichiri Beach in Sagami Province"

Wild Word: "Tea House at Koishikawa, the Morning after a Snowfall" and "Yoshida at Tōkaidō"

Willawaw Journal: "Ejiri in Suruga Province"; "Nihonbashi Bridge in Edo"; "Tsukuda Island in Musashi Province"; "Under Mannen Bridge at Fukagawa"; and "Ushibori in Hitachi Province"

"Sunset across the Ryōgoku Bridge from the Bank of the Sumida River at Onmayagashi" was a Finalist in the *Naugatuck River Review* 11th Annual Narrative Poetry Contest (2020)

Preface

The thirty-six woodblock prints that were the inspiration for this collection of writings were made by **Katsushika Hokusai** (葛飾 北斎 | 1760–1849). The pieces show different views of Mount Fuji from various waystations where people would go to look at the beautiful mountain. Standing at about twelve thousand feet above sea level, Mount Fuji is located roughly sixty miles southwest of Tokyo, and can be seen from the city on clear days.

The writings in this book are haibun, a literary form originating in Japan. **Matsuo Basho** (松尾 芭蕉 | 1644–1694), famous for his haiku, was the first to use the term for this style of writing, which combines prose—autobiography, diary entries, essay, or short story—and poetry—often haiku.

Basho wrote some haibun while traveling, the most famous of which is ***Narrow Road to the Interior*** (奥の細道 | **Oku no Hosomichi**). It is very likely that Hokusai would have been familiar with this popular work.

Hokusai was in his seventies when he produced the Mount Fuji series; the author, Martin Willitts Jr., was seventy years old when he began studying the prints, attempting to merge himself with Hokusai.

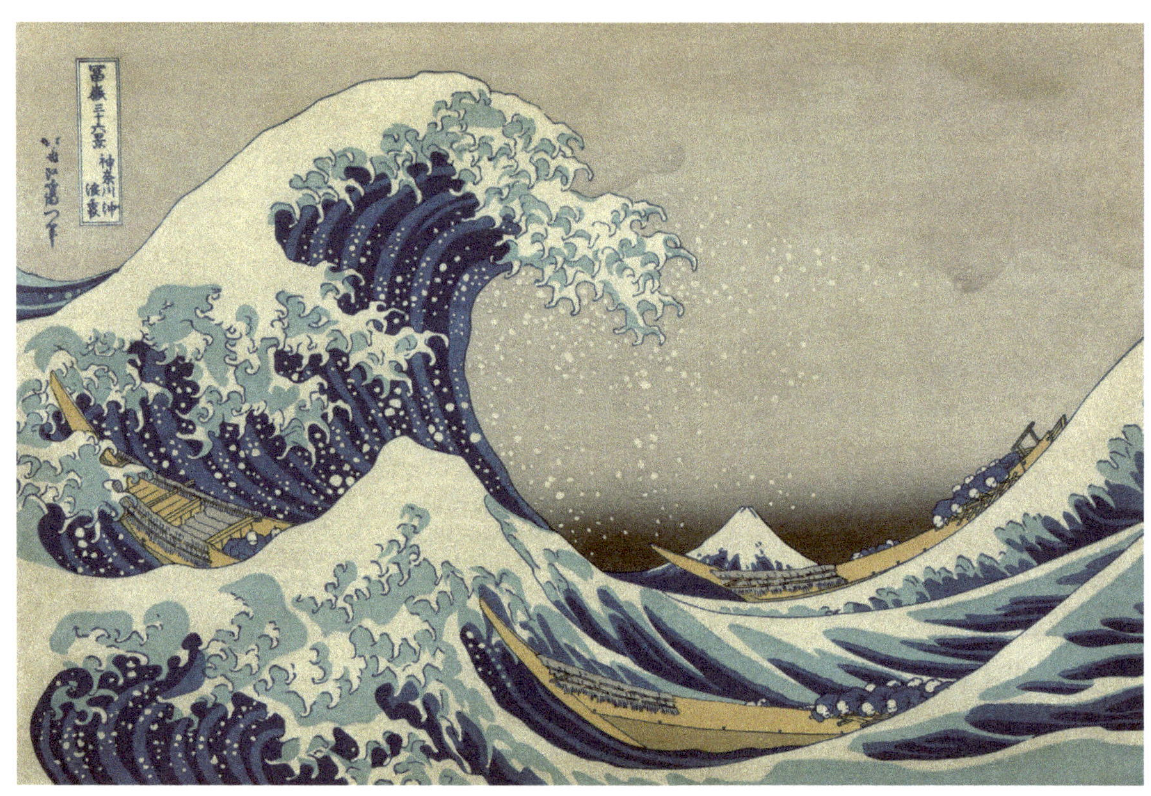

日本語: 神奈川沖浪裏 (Kanagawa-oki nami-ura)

The Great Wave off Kanagawa

I do not want to intrude where I do not belong; however, I have to follow an urge, a great tidal wave I call Love. I must discover and relearn the world before it changes again, forming larger and larger into a tsunami. If I hurry and take my time, I can paint with new love. Everywhere I will go, I will notice what is happening and what is not happening. In the silence or among the crisp noises, in the drowning light or pitching waves of darkness, I must find out what is important and what is insignificant. I have to see the unseen, hear the voiceless, embracing sweltering color and light within love, and experience the calmness afterward.

Love is heading toward Mount Fuji, shoved back by uncontrollable waves. I cannot control the wind, the way the world goes from dark to light and back again, or the amount of time a snail crawls across a leaf.

How quickly the washes of color change the sky; and still, it looks as clear as water! Mount Fuji cannot do anything about the weather, either.

The world knows changes can be good, bad, or indifferent. Some invisible paintbrush is moving the color of waves. During the violence of waves, there is no sound before, too much sound during, then silence after ships are broken into pieces, floating like plum petals on a stilled pond.

My hand sketches this scene. Love tilts along with the sun setting into the ocean. The sky cries for help and mercy. Ships are caught and released, caught and released, caught and released.

Waves toss boats as leaves.
The sun never sets on dew
in a plum blossom.

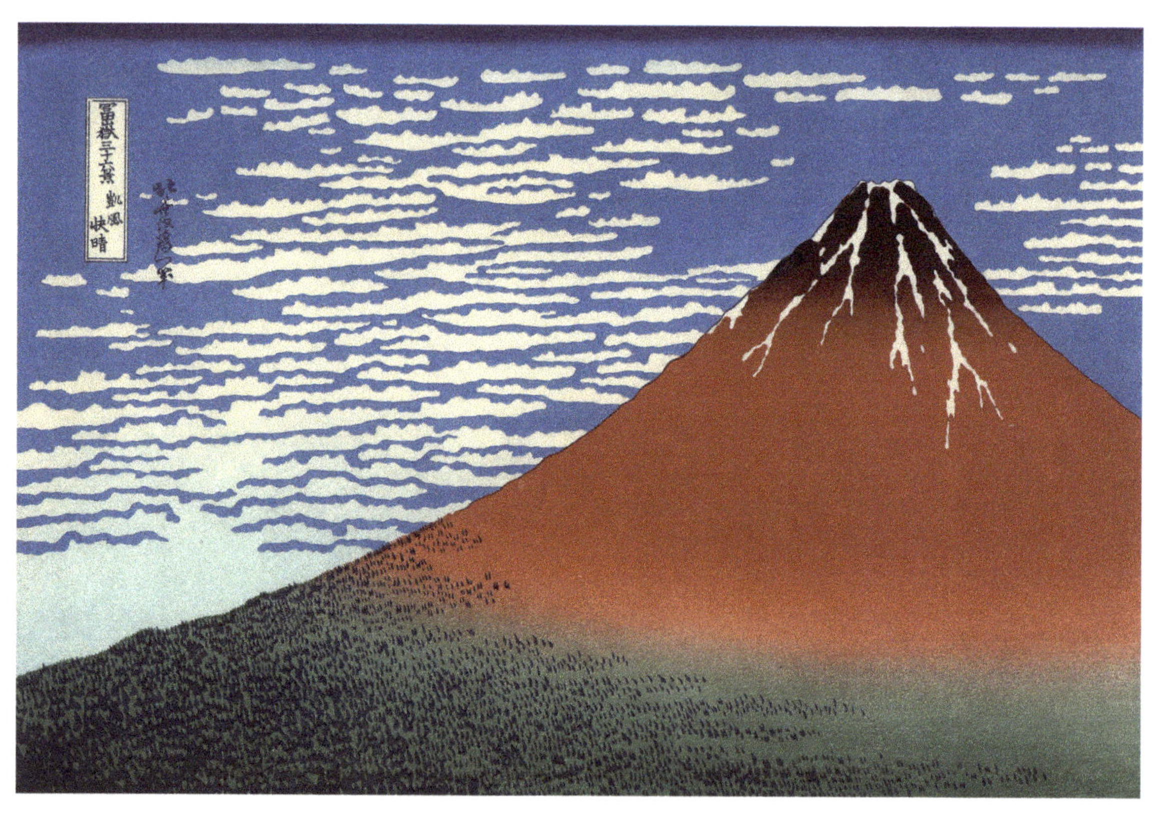

日本語: 凱風快晴 (Gaifū kaisei)

South Wind, Clear Sky (Red Fuji)

Geese unravel white ribbons everywhere, streaking across the sky. Monks try to clear a path of stones, while other monks sweep the stones back. The south wind barks like a dog. Couples throw plates in anger. Birds gush-away for winter. Spiders scatter before a broom catches them. The clouds are gone. My mind was already scattered in that last wind.

All this energy is unsettling the world. It is all useless activity.

Mount Fuji settles into the hot sunset, an afterimage blending into the water, a red glow diminishing like a woman's nipple.

My wife is waiting for me, calling from distance and separation. When I finally will return, I hope her sadness will part as curtains. Her happiness will be wind chimes, and my hands will paint all over her body. Geese will splash up into the blank sky.

Red Fuji at night—
the eyes of cranes settling,
never see enough.

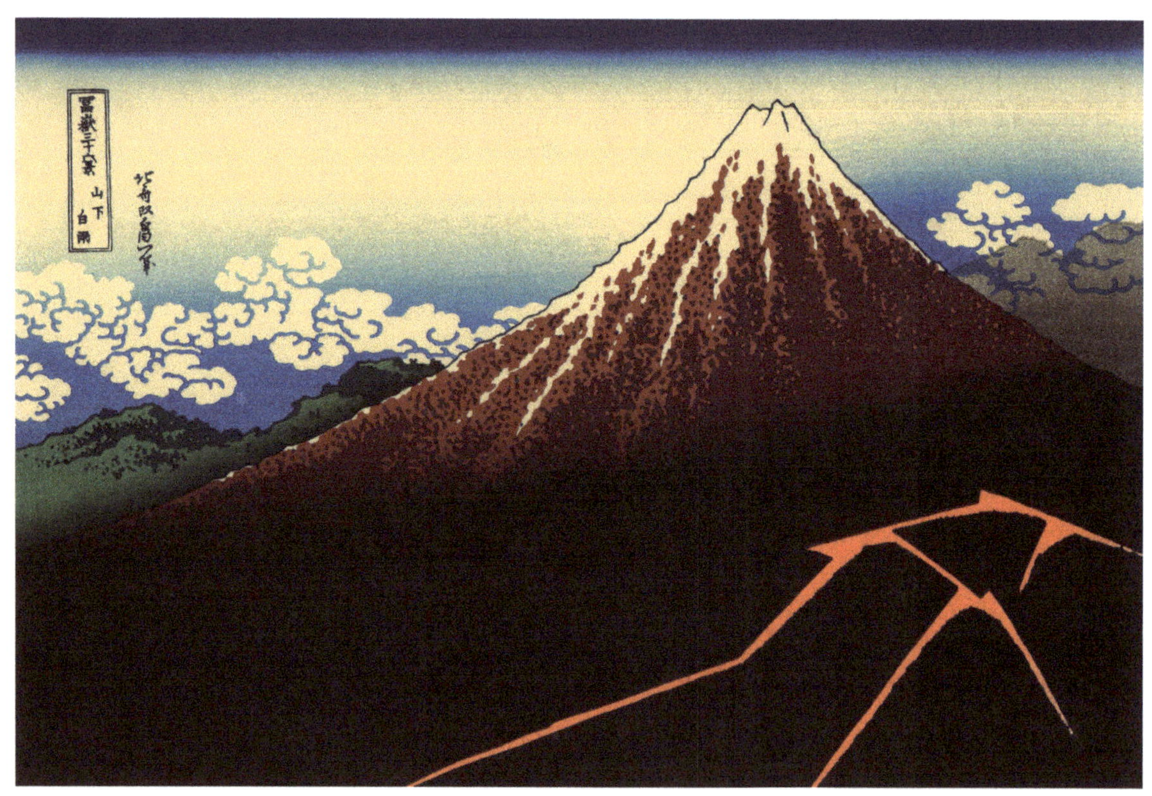

日本語: 山下白雨 (Sanka hakū)

Rainstorm Beneath the Summit

Mount Fuji dances, lifts her foot, the ground moving and shaking, and trees shimmer. She is dancing to the flute of a birdcall, unable to control how she is affected by love.

The wind is excited. It has waited too long to dance with the mountain. A reaction is building. Enlarged dark clouds are puffing from the wind's chest. The wind can only resist so much temptation. The air is vibrating. Mount Fuji tempts the clouds. Rain spills out of wind, drenching the mountain with vibrant, fluent music.

I hear my wife singing to the birds in a garden rainstorm. The birds respond, composing a song.

When my wife removes her robe and her naked flesh is the color of white cherry blossoms, I have the same lack of restraint as the wind. I rain, many times, dabs of paint, sprinkles, huge cloudbursts, lightning everywhere.

Rain after a burst
collects on a white rose bud.
Fuji rocks glisten.

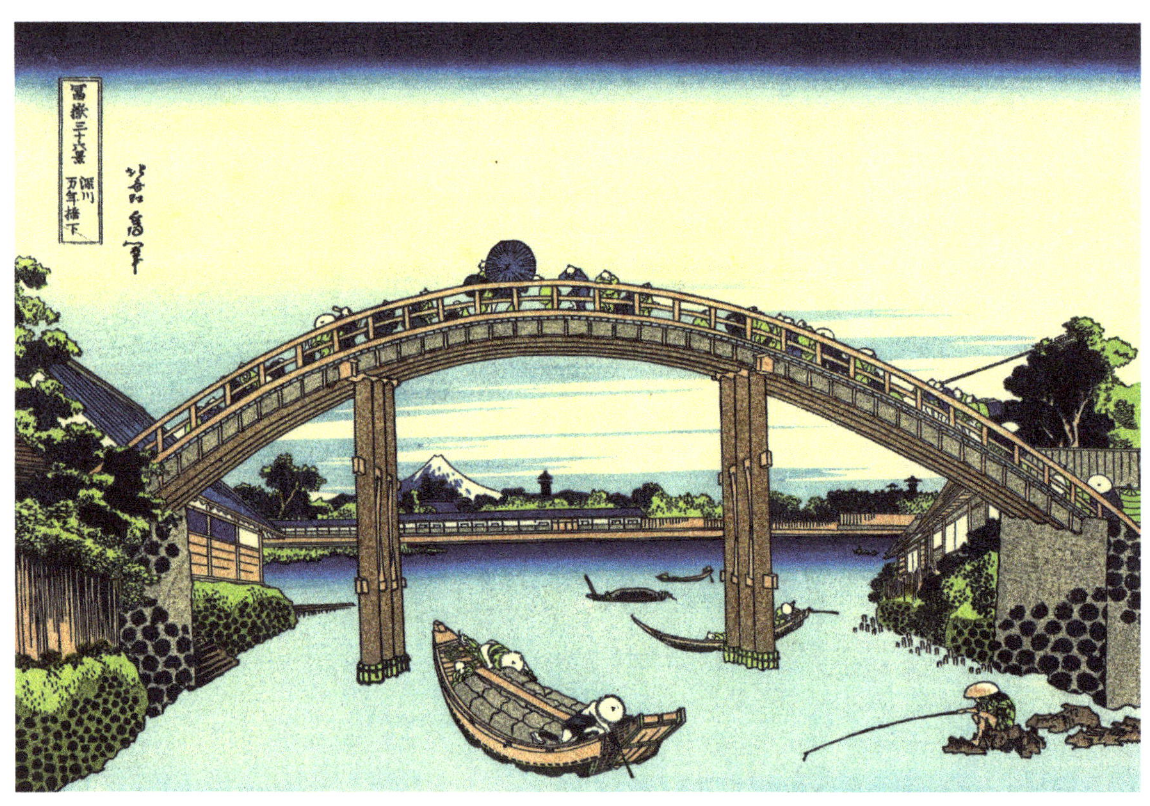

日本語: 深川万年橋下 (Fukagawa Mannen-bashi shita)

Print Four

Under Mannen Bridge at Fukagawa

Travelers meet each other in the middle of the bridge and pass each other like centipedes. No one watches where he or she is going. Some people pass through each other like ghosts in a hurry to find new bodies.

People are always in a hurry to get nowhere fast; they never notice the bridge is a frown over the river. Always, people are going from side to side, as impatient as fleas. They never look at Mount Fuji over their shoulder. These people have no time for love.

Under the bridge, a boat sets out to find the source of the sun. A man fishes but fish do not notice the bait. Mount Fuji feels ignored. It has been here before there were people crossing the bridge, before the river under the bridge, before trees, before the bridge.

I think about how a bridge always leads toward love.

I want to make a picture to please the world. I merge brush and paper, becoming a bridge between eye and hand. My heart launches many boats of love under the bridge, fishing for lovers.

Nothing to eat.
I eat imagination
one grain at a time.

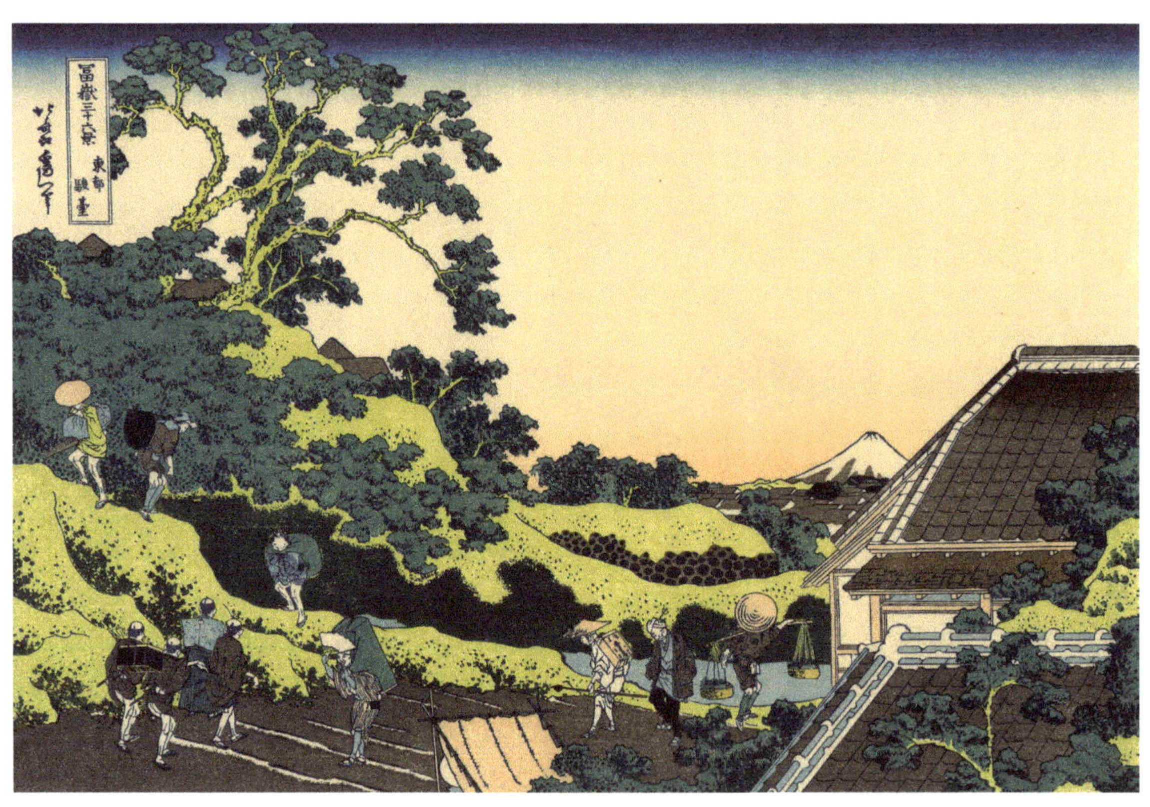

日本語: 東都駿台 (Tōto sundai)

Sundai in Edo

Birds bring mystery to music.

Carrying bags of dirt and stone has tilted men's bodies. A large pine tree squiggles against the sky. The shogun's retainers fill a mansion. At this elevation, we can all see the city of Edo; but all I hear is the music of love.

A corner of a gray-tiled roof tries to block my view of Mount Fuji in the distance. The highlands gradually rise from the center of my viewpoint, and at the top of the hill are more trees. This creates a dip in the center of the world, but I listen for the love that creates music.

Men carry box-shaped luggage on their backs, ascending and descending the hill. I can imagine anything I want inside the boxes—none of the boxes belongs to me. If I open one of the boxes, I might find a blue roof tile, a bag of soil and stones, or the scent of Edo. But what I want to find when I open every box is music and love.

At this height, I have a shadow like any samurai. My shadow moves pine tree branches. The world sags and swells, drifting temporary shadows. My shadow loves to play with the music, as if the notes were birds perching and resting on my hands.

No one reaches Fuji by traveling on this road, but my brush will. I paint with the mystery of bird music.

On a tree near sky
I open clouds of boxes.
What might be inside?

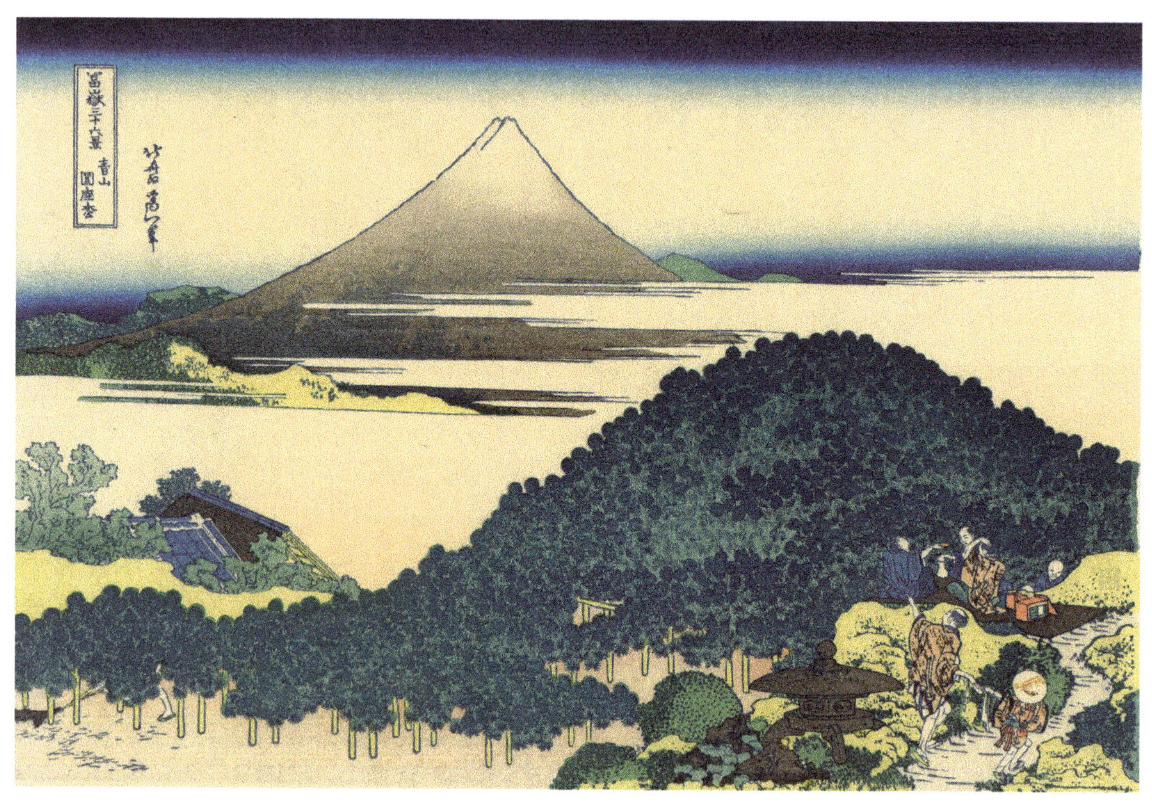

日本語: 青山円座松 (Aoyama enza-no-matsu)

Cushion Pine at Aoyama

At the garden of Ryüganji, an enormous green cushion pine tree is perfect to sit on and contemplate this Zen temple. Some branches are forty feet long and cannot hold their own immeasurable weight, so stilts as strong as crane legs hold them up in a monsoon season.

Picnickers enjoy the day. Their conversation is green tea leaves being stirred. The mountain is pleased that people can know quiet peace somewhere in this fragile world; otherwise, a monsoon could blow us all away with dandelion puffs.

A father and son join two men drinking sake and sitting on a rug. When I try to ask these strangers to share the sake, they chase me away with unkind words. This is not the garden of love. Didn't the masters talk about sharing?

Mount Fuji is frowning. She knows what I say is true. Truth nests like a stork.

If only the Mount Fuji had journeyed with me, we could have talked softly as pine needles. We could have been searching together for someone willing to give an old man a sip of sake or find someone to give me color for a paintbrush.

My wife waits for me, holding a green bowl filled with leek soup, love floating in the broth.

Pine branches stretching
after a long winter nap
try to hug Fuji.

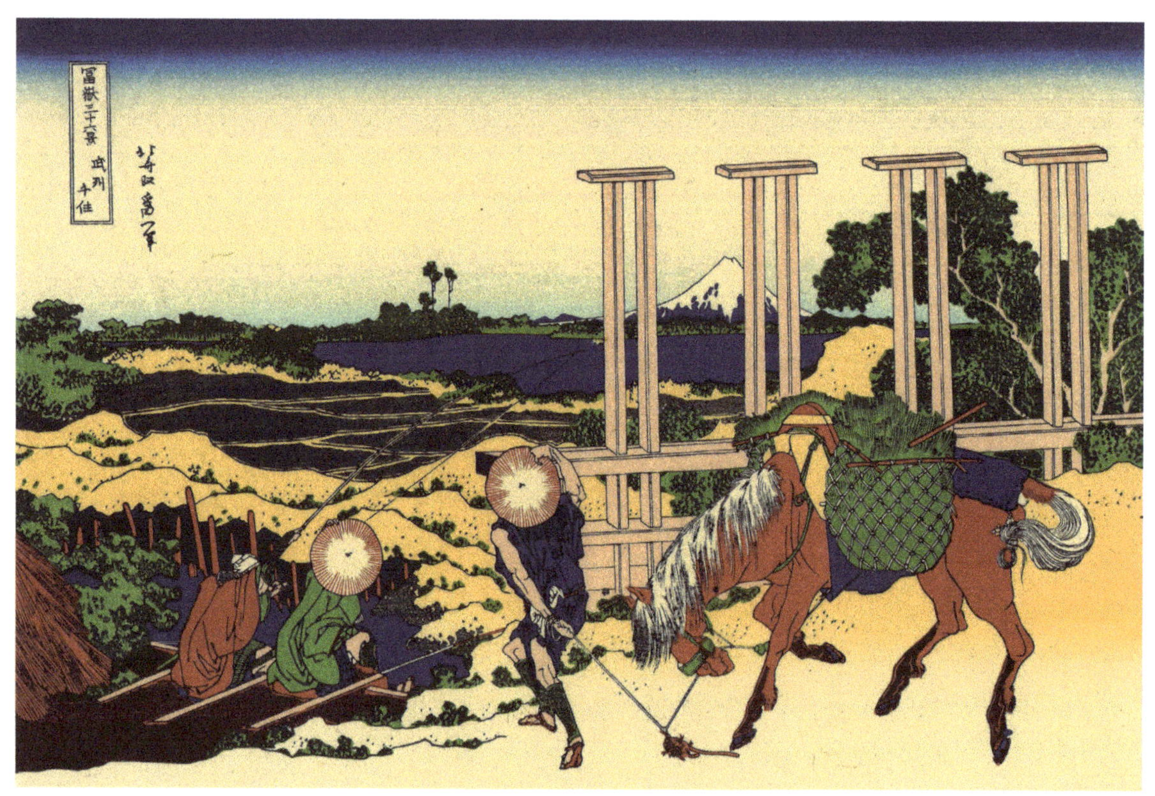

日本語: 武州千住 (Bushū Senju)

Print Seven

Senju, Musashi Province

A worker tries to lead a horse where the horse refuses to go. He can yank all he wants, but the horse does not want to move. Life is frustrating when nothing does what we want it to do. Love can get as stubborn as a horse sitting, refusing to budge. Love is wanting us to move in the same direction, but sometimes we resist. We cannot force love, or horses, or weather.

Two excited men are searching for some hidden secrets in this marsh. I know they will find nothing because I already looked, and my hands are empty hollow reeds. We have nothing if we do not have love. Love gallops ahead without us.

Fishermen can throw out their nets and retrieve only seaweed and water. A peasant woman at a loom can miss a stitch, and the whole cloth could unravel. Love takes much hard work, and failure is always possible.

All I think about is how far I am from Mount Fuji and how far I am from home. My wife is turning over in her sleep, and as her robe parts, a rose petal appears: where am I?

I carry dreams from my head to my hands to paper. I try to paint what I miss.

Useless small breezes
open days as cherry blossoms.
We are hungry bees.

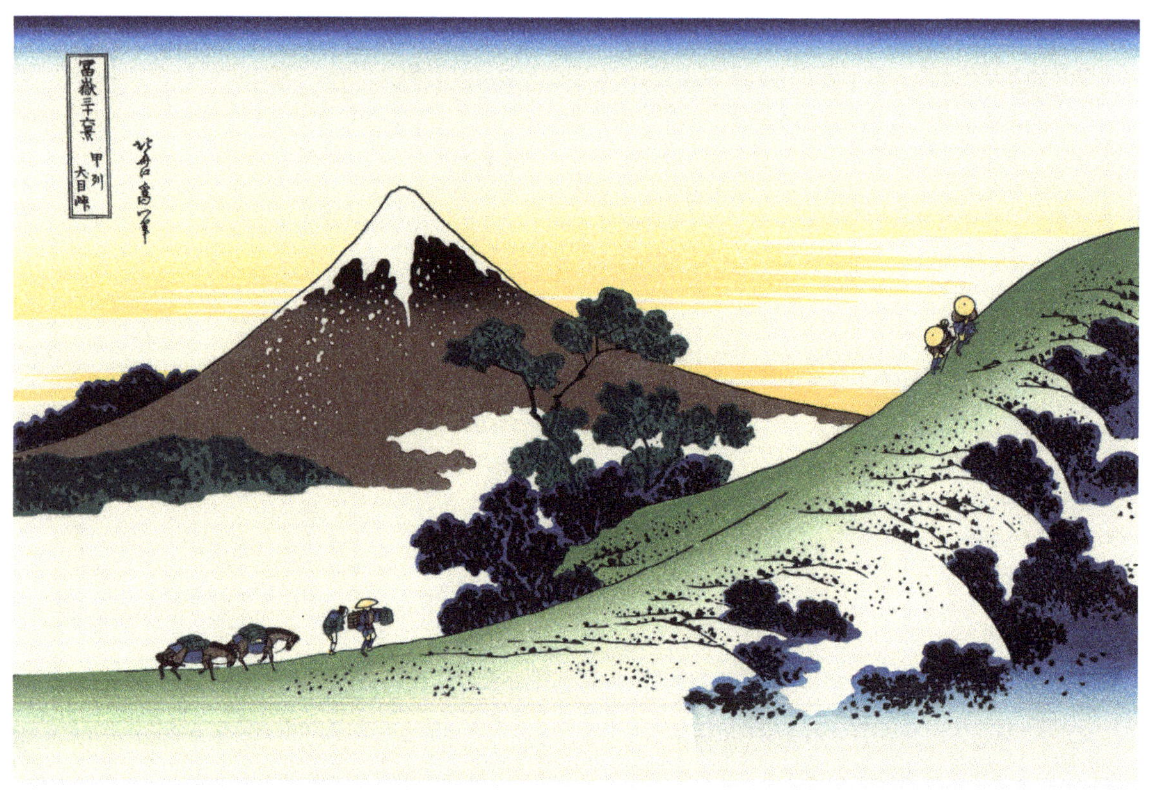

日本語: 甲州犬目峠 (Kōshū inume-tōge)

PRINT EIGHT

Inume Pass, Kōshū

You can travel your entire life to Mount Fuji and never reach it. Whenever you are near Mount Fuji, you will find yourself back at the beginning of your journey. You could lose yourself in dreams, and you would never reach Mount Fuji. Dreams are less than steam from a teapot.

Men with horses are starting up the hill. For them, the hill is just beginning. It is hot, and they climb into the heat. The horses are smart enough to know they do not want to start this late in the day. The impossible is just beginning. Those men do not know they are seeing themselves almost getting nowhere. Mount Fuji has sent them back again. Time splits and separates us from ourselves. Where is the beginning and where is the end? Maybe there is neither.

The mountain is saying, You cannot go any further; you must try again.

I heard that same message from my wife when she was interested, and I was still too tired from last night's lovemaking. We chased each other with the same ambition of squirrels. A teapot can make steam; I cannot.

Spring footprints on trees,
on hills, on rivers, on clouds—
squirrels in crazy-love.

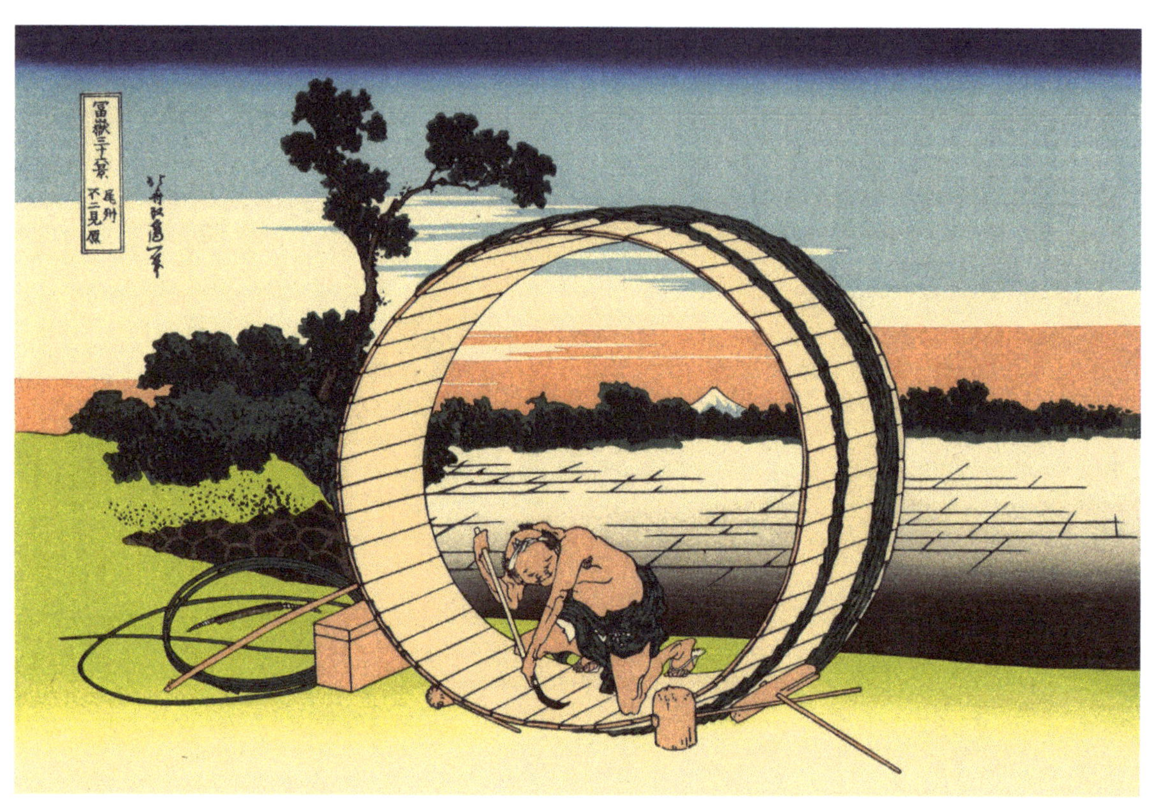

日本語: 尾州不二見原 (Bishū Fujimigahara)

PRINT NINE

Fuji View Field in Owari Province

A barrel-maker was in the middle of a barrel, bending the large, wet wood into a hoop. He must have patience and skill. In a world of barrels, someone has to make them.

I asked him if this barrel would hold water or sake. Neither, he groaned, forcing it into shape. One good wind, and he might roll across the fields in that circle.

The barrel shape was a giant eye seeing Mount Fuji in the center.

Small ants were mounding dirt, preparing for a storm. The ants sense rain is coming before leaves fluster and rend. And if the emergency departs before it arrives, the ants will disassemble the mound, each grain of dirt after grain of dirt.

We cannot control nature. We can only prepare. A barrel can catch rain. A sumo can try to hold back storms with his hands, but the wind will push back. The only certainty is uncertainty.

In a world full of barrels, what would you place inside of one? I would place love. We could drink endlessly until we were filled.

Ants make a large mound—
rain—soon a barrel will fill—
circle completed.

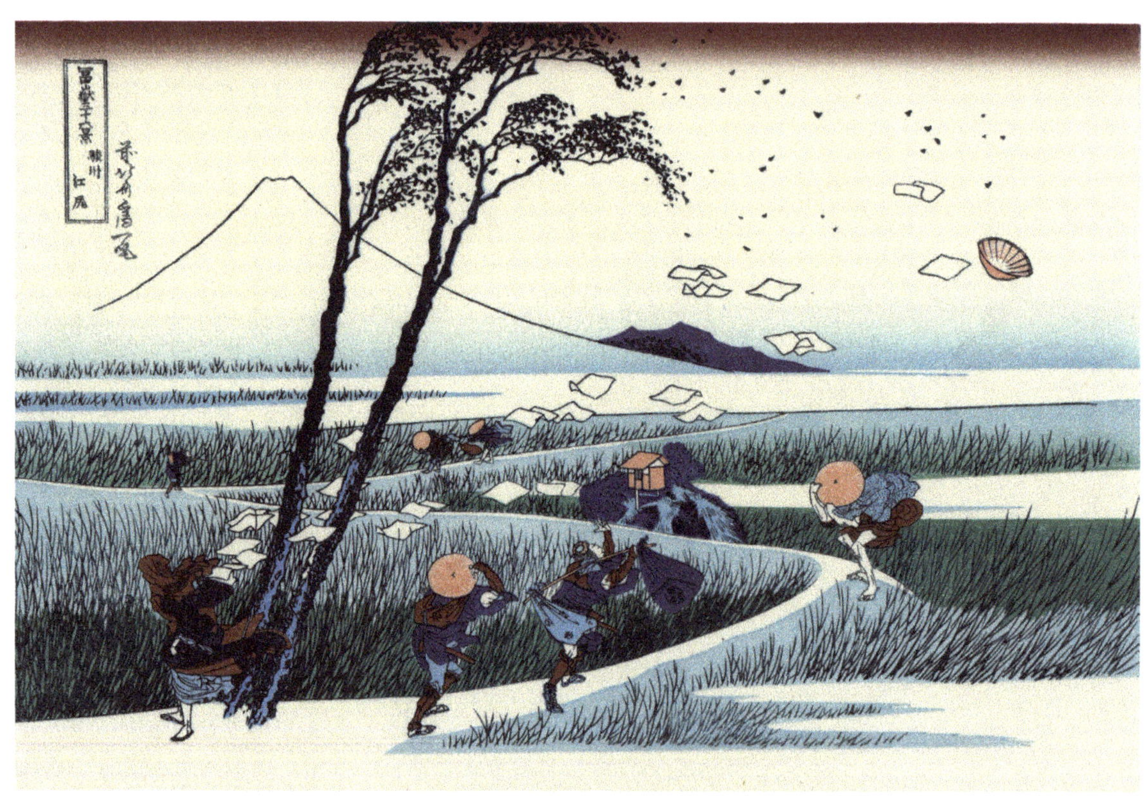

日本語: 駿州江尻 (Sunshū Ejiri)

Ejiri in Suruga Province

A surprising, annoying squall astonishes the travelers on the paper road. The storm snarls through marsh. Wind takes parts of soil, moss, tree bark, haiku, and a man's hat. Now he must chase both the hat and his frustration. Other travelers face the wind, crouching low, clinging to their hats.

Hundreds of blank papers whirl as doves out of a woman's backpack. Wind upsurges, scattering rice paper for miles, and the ground can now write the story of its life, composing days of sun and shade, or rains in the beginning of spring, or snow on empty branches. Love can scatter this easily.

When we do not hang onto life, it often blows away. Love can be that elusive, so we hold it tight.

Wind covers the woman's face with her own coat. She cannot see how the paper disappeared. She does not see the tall trees lose their leaves, falling as sparks. Love, sometimes, is what we cannot see, but feel.

On the Tökaidö Road, I choose to paint this inconspicuous spot in Ejiri, focused on the insistent wind. Mount Fuji remains white and unshaken, affected neither by wind nor by human problems.

On a clear day, I can see the three volcanoes of Mount Fuji. The volcanoes can be the entrance of heaven or hell, depending on your point of view. Climbing the mountain is a sign of devotion. At my age and poverty, I cannot afford to make that journey, so I am making thirty-six views of Fuji using my brushes and paints, swishing colors in the wind. Love is knowing what we can do within our limits and understanding when we cannot match each other's expectations.

Wind wrinkles the earth,
my ragged clothes, paper and paint.
Only Fuji stands.

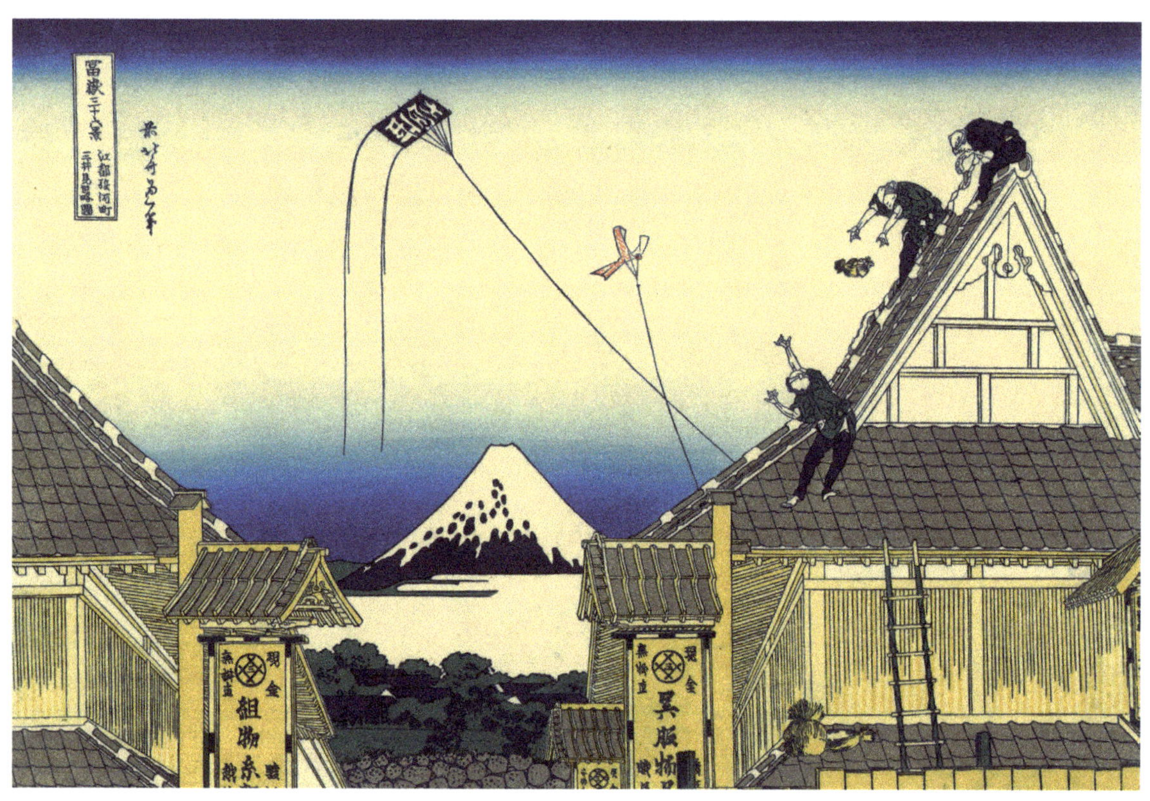

日本語: 江都駿河町三井見世略図 (Kōto Suruga-cho Mitsui Miseryakuzu)

A Sketch of the Mitsui Shop in Suruga in Edo

Sometimes, you begin with a simple plan.

Miso soup has become money in the Mitsui shop in Edo. This is an unusual way to deal with business. I do not have any money to exchange. Lack of money is not a good plan.

I tried to give the shopkeeper some moonlight in exchange for food, but he laughs at my offering. Instead, I begin sketching this building while men begin working on the roof. Over time, they will finish before I do. It takes me a long time to find a good place to stand. The sun is especially hot when I cannot afford shade.

There are two kites trying to mate in mid-air. I am sad because I never tried that with my wife when we were young as clouds.

It costs more to stand still and paint than it does to dream about my wife, ruffling her kimono as I loosen the obi from her waist, releasing it to the wind, abandoned like kite strings.

I came without money, and I will leave rich with love. Even as an old man, past the midnight of his life, I can still find the wonder of my wife. No money can buy love. No miso soup is a fair exchange. Love is always the better, simpler plan.

Kites find breeze in sun,
workers nail moonlight to roof,
I select wife's hand.

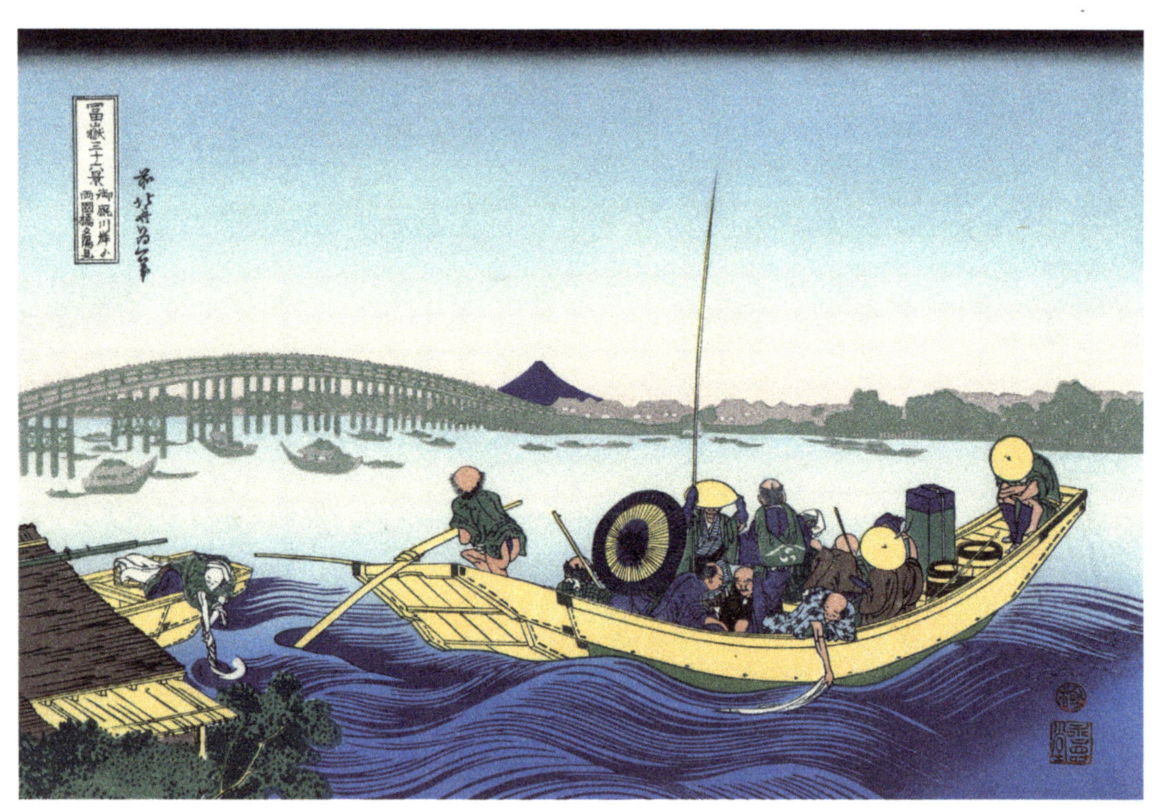

日本語: 御厩川岸より両国橋夕陽見 (Ommayagashi yori ryōgoku-bashi yūhi mi)

Sunset across the Ryōgoku Bridge from the Bank of the Sumida River at Onmayagashi

Ten people are on a boat crossing the Sumida River. The boat sinks low to the water. If the boat sinks any more, the passengers will be in the river, drowning, and then they will appear down river like dead carp. An old man with a patch of black hair surrounding his bald head is pushing the boat through the stilled river with a long pole.

What is it like to be rich enough to cross the Ryōgoku Bridge? The bridge spans from shore to shore on wooden pilings. I hear a grasshopper leaping on the plank boards. More boats enter and leave under the bridge. Some boats are heading to one shore with hesitation. Some boats depart to other destinations in the distant horizon. Mount Fuji waits for everyone to settle down.

I have a choice. I can cross to the village on the other side, or I can stay here. At either place, I will be sleeping outside with the crickets. Mosquitoes will be telling me the news of my future, and I will slap them away, not wanting to hear the inevitable. One woman is washing her laundry in the river. I see her twist dark-blue water, wringing the cloth. The sun's reflection follows one boat into the starless night. A passenger at the prow is asleep. Today has the calmness of my wife when she accepts my foolishness.

I do not understand the quiet of a river. A splash could be a fish. Or that splash could be a man dipping his hand to feel the movement of water against his hand. Or a splash could be small gasps of sunset floating on the river. But I have seen the calm. It is my wife shrugging her shoulders as if to say, *Foolish, foolish man, what will I do with you?*

Stars are sleeping fish.
No one disturbs quiet boats.
No frog-splash rippling.

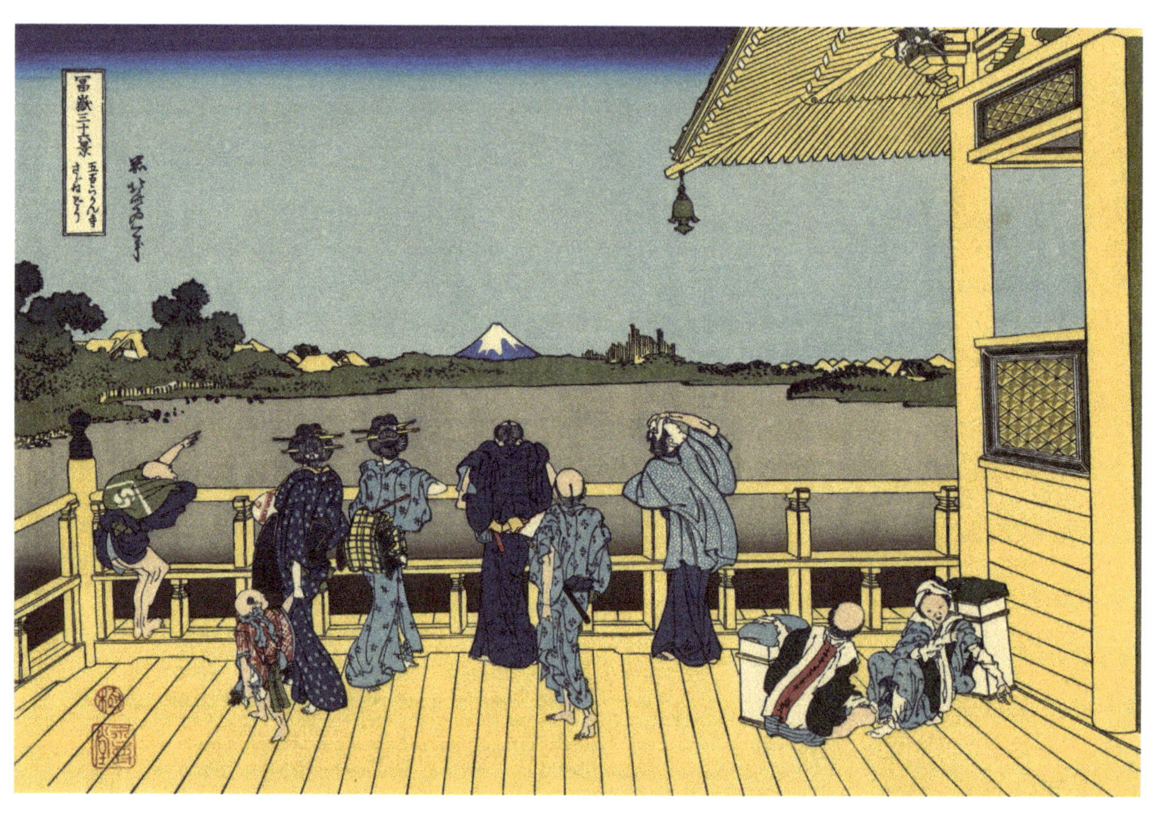

日本語: 五百らかん寺さざるどう (Gohyaku-rakanji Sazaidō)

Sazai Hall—Temple of Five Hundred Rakan

I miss my wife's face in the endless dark. That first time I held her hand, clouds of geese thundered overhead. Now, loss follows me as shadows. Her face is the moon wandering in the sky, but I cannot reach her. I miss the air she breathes.

On the balcony of the Sazaidō, I joined the others to see Mount Fuji. I climbed the spiral staircase of the three-story tower, counting each step. Each one takes me further from the beginning.

I was not getting any closer to Mount Fuji than I was getting closer to my wife. Shadows stay below the stairs.

A tiny bell hangs from the edge of the temple roof. The legendary disciples of Buddha hung this bell with such care, out of reach of any man, so only the Divine could ring it. Not even a fierce wind can disturb the bell's silence.

The absence of the bell ringing is also the impossibility of hearing morning light stirring, my wife opening a window, a meadow lark in the forest shadows.

If that bell saw my wife combing her long hair, spilling like waves, the bell would ring endlessly!

The rest of this world heads toward the vanishing point only an artist can see. A shadow depends on the presence or absence of light.

Yesterday: too long
since we said farewell. It rains,
helping birds find worms.

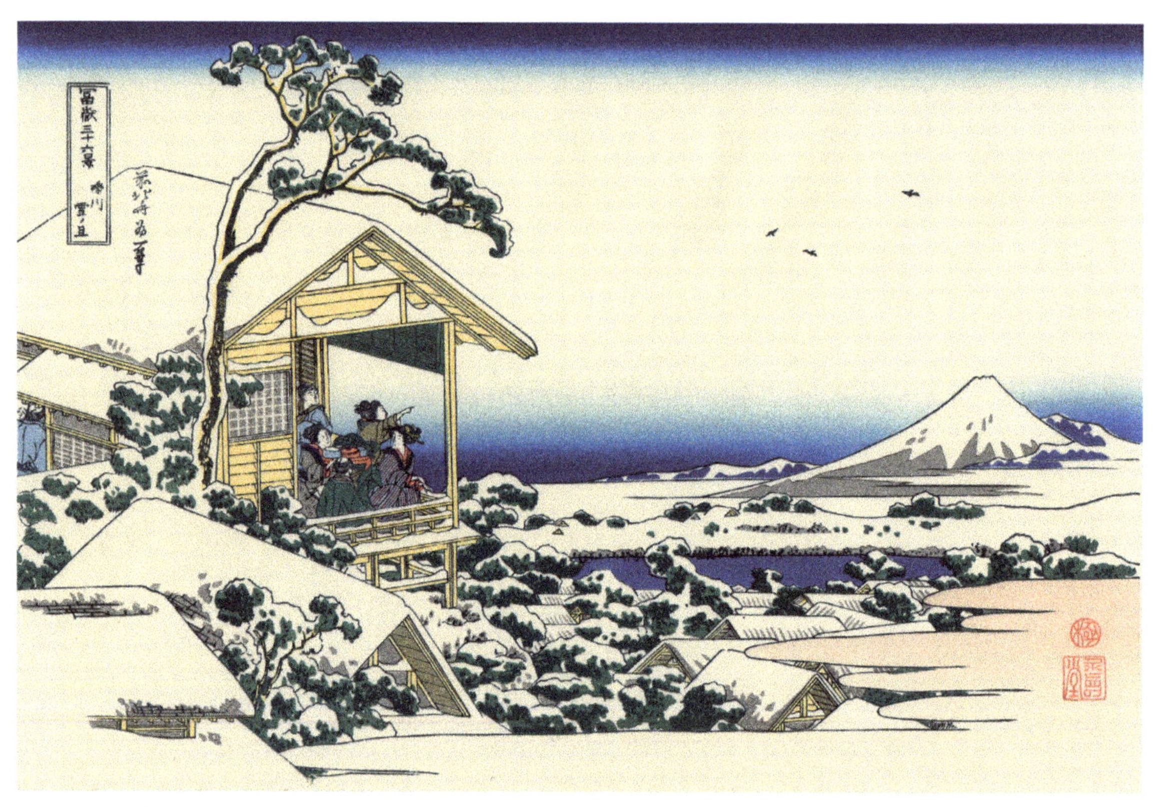

日本語: 礫川雪の旦 (Koishikawa yuki no ashita)

Tea House at Koishikawa, the Morning after a Snowfall

Excited people at the tea house point toward Mount Fuji, quieted by snow. White edges are everywhere. I hold one flake on my hand as it melts, giving into the heat from my palm; but for a moment, it was the same weight as the first time holding our baby. All life is temporary as tea steam, but we can try to cradle memory.

Long shadows stretch between the generations of my family, and now those shadows are covered with softness. See how memory melts. All morning, light fills footprints in snow with blue shadows, continuous silences, elusive snow flexing its quiet intent. Snow is giggling in the air. Snow is the color of my beard and remaining hair. Snow is the memory of cherry blossoms. Snow is the stillness of cranes trying to stand on uncertain ice. Steam rises from water as tea kettle mist. I cannot see my wife in the clouds or reflections of snow.

Each day shortens during winter. Then days increase their steps toward spring. What do I know of permanence? I went on a journey without my wife, and now her memory swirls as snowflakes in the indecisive winds. Even Mount Fuji does not know what to say this morning. Instead, Fuji chooses meditation. It goes silent, accepting the chill and snow. It merges with snow, steam, silence, cranes, wind.

People on this balcony are pointing to the mountain. Cranes open white wings, fly off chasing the sun. My breath flies with them to the mountain. The cranes sing with my wife's voice when she greets me. I am off on this journey, sketching these images, quick as each flake. I miss that sound, that morning-waking call of my wife, excited about the smallest moments.

I drop my paintbrush. Feathers bristle against my painting. I feel the invisible. A snowflake reddens my cheek, a wife's kiss.

Snow softens all sounds
until less than your poured tea
or feather drifting.

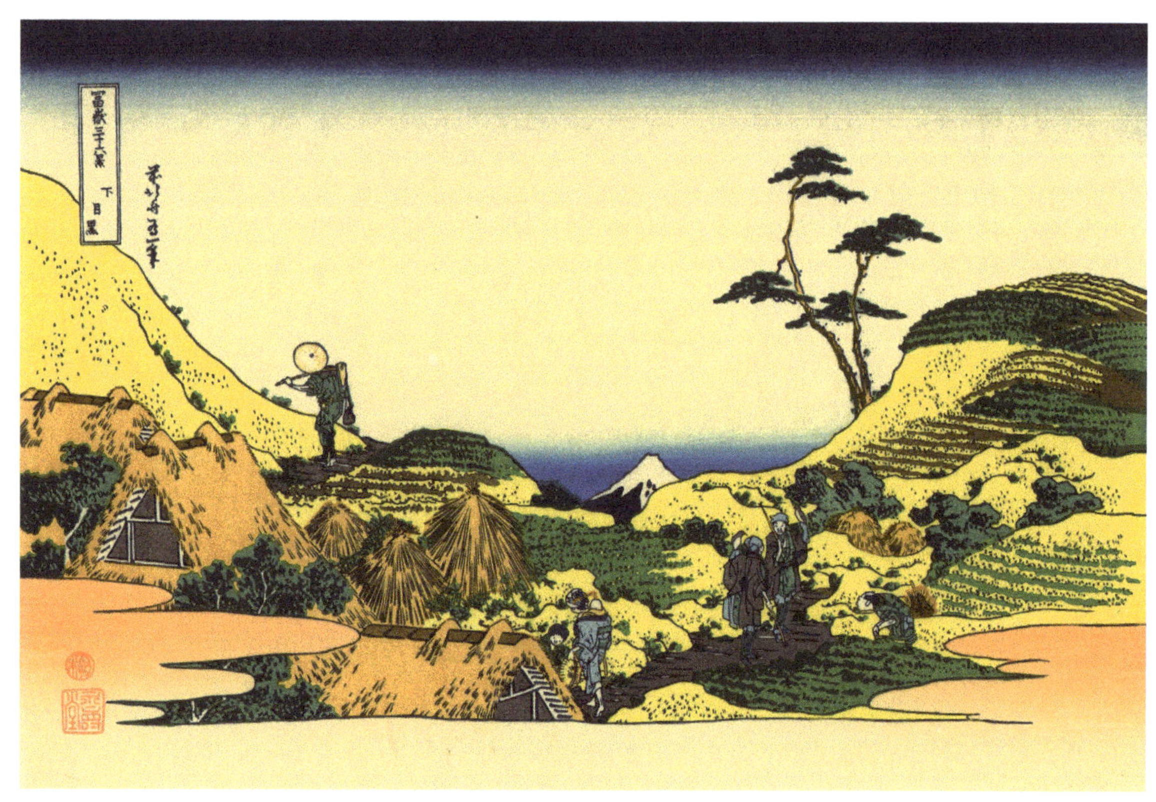

日本語: 下目黒 (Shimo-Meguro)

Below Meguro

How much protection from sun, wind, rain, and snow can these straw-thatched roofs provide to these poor villagers? Little more than sleeping in the open, like me. I wake up in a blanket of snow. I must continue my journey around Mount Fuji. It is the only way back to my wife. Life can be as short as a gong.

We are all headed somewhere. We never know what we will discover on the way. Whatever is happening ahead already changes and changes again. Whatever we leave behind changes, too, in the retelling. The world has impermanent memory. We no sooner arrive, we are leaving.

One man is leaving. His bundle sways with the beginning of a long journey. Grass is short at the start of spring, and it will grow while he travels. When he gets further on the road, will he regret leaving? What is he leaving behind? I already regret my traveling and holding this picture in my hands. I miss my wife. Why did I leave her behind? The past is already being reconstructed.

The man is leaving, headed toward the unknown. The unknown is expecting him. His shadow remains at the house, still holding a hoe after planting. His shadow rests on a handmade bench. His shadow is tired after seasons of planting, and it is too sore to go to bed. His shadow is too exhausted to join his body. His shadow has fallen asleep, dreaming of purple cabbage heads, round as the sun or clouds over Fuji.

My wife is waiting for me, through seasons, under a straw-thatched roof. I tried to leave my shadow behind, but it followed me this far. I cannot send it back. I have tried. My shadow sways a bundle of sorrow, regretting every mile. It wants to kick me for leaving. My shadow stares back to my house, trying to see my wife. I left over seventeen drawings ago. My life is a clenched fistful of straw.

We all leave something of ourselves behind.

I have this one truth:
no one can break a fistful
of straw, easily.

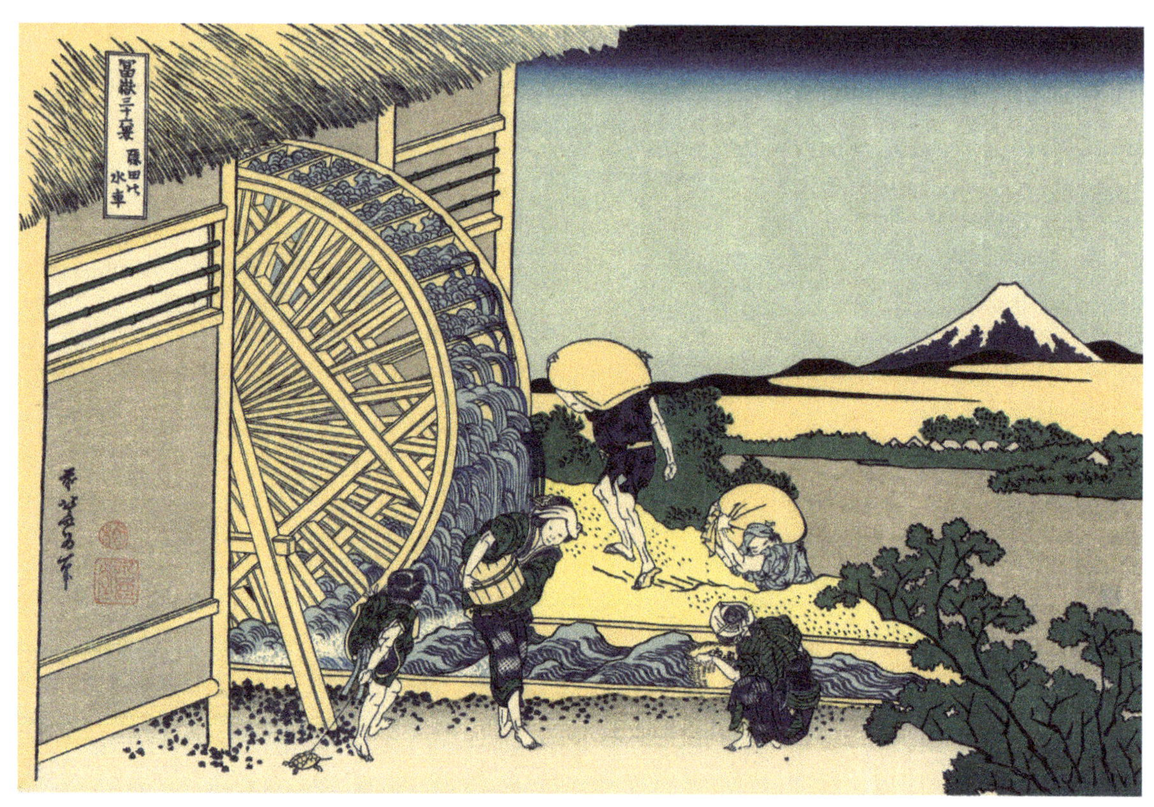

日本語: 隠田の水車 (Onden no suisha)

Watermill at Ondenv

The wheel rotates water into a slide. Women take buckets away while other women are bringing empty buckets. The wheel brings water regardless if anyone takes any water away.

Men carry sacks of wheat to be ground into smaller grain. The wheel rolls over the grain in another circle, churned by the water. As the water turns, so does the wheel. The wheel crushes the wheat almost into dust. The wheel never stops. The number of men carrying bags never stops. The water never stops.

The sun follows the moon on a bridge as it crosses over the sky.

This world has motions this repetitive. This is useless pursuit. Not even Mount Fuji can explain why. I am dizzy watching this turning activity.

Is it possible for a day to avoid following another day by skipping the endless cycle of days?

My paintbrush makes small, tight circles: Light and Dark walk on the same circular path around Mount Fuji, wearing it down.

This world is a grain
carried in a sack, then ground
into fine laughter.

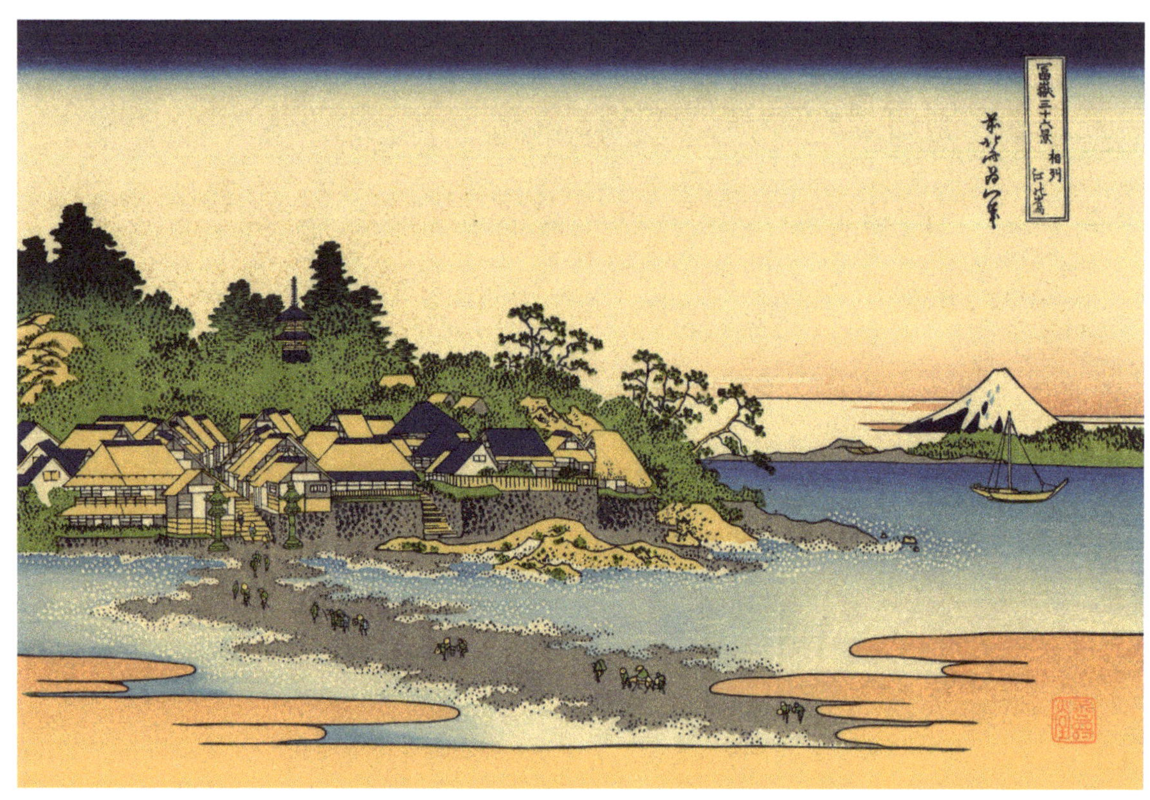

日本語: 相州江の島 (Soshū Enoshima)

Enoshima in Sagami Province

From the mud flats facing toward the village, steps lead up steep cliffs to the houses on the edge. If those houses were to get close to the edge, they might have the urge to jump off into the shallow shoreline. Heat wavers on the firmness of house tops.

I have not moved from my vantage spot on a high hill under the shade of a plum tree. My attention is not on the people as sometimes their ankles sink in mud and sand. Nor do I care about the sailboat passing across the front of Mount Fuji. My eyes do not follow the trees leaning toward the sea. Neither do I focus on the temple poking through the disruption of trees beyond the houses. I think, glancingly, of my wife, and I am distracted. I cannot focus on this spiritual journey around the thirty-six waiting spots to view Mount Fuji. When I write this journal, my words are loose mud; not one firm word rising to the surface like a heat wave. My words purple and bruise with all this disappointment and regret. Words leap off the page, sketches shift like shadows in wind. The unstable world is shaking loose all our footsteps.

My ankles are tired from standing as still as a crane on this sandy hill. I just want to fly off to snatch fish in the shallows. Or swoop back home to my wife's arms. Or find a vantage point to create my pictures. I might as well climb a steep cliff.

Above me, there is enough light from the morning star to share with this shade tree.

In this world, it is possible to be apart from people and still be close to people. It is the same as dew being everywhere on every object. It is the same as the watery memory of my wife, entering and ebbing, entering, ebbing.

Shadows jump off cliffs.
The sun is caught in wet sand,
stranded as a fish.

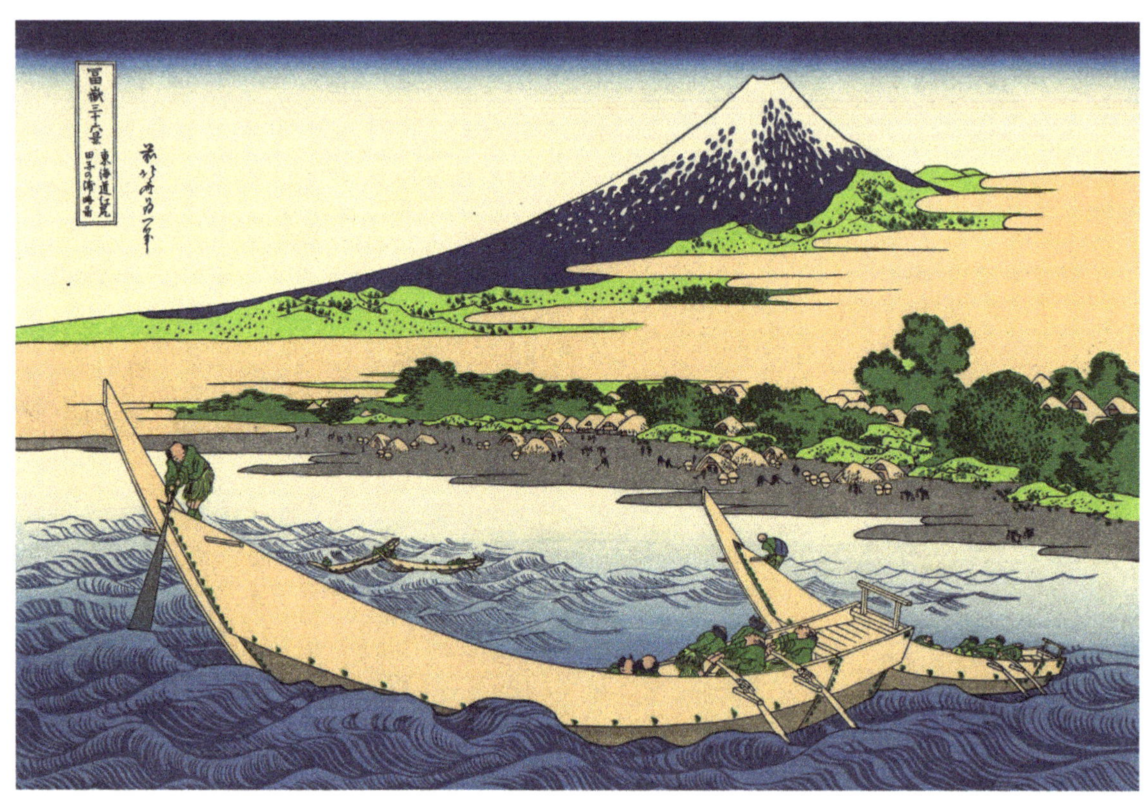

日本語: 東海道江尻田子の浦略図 (Tōkaidō Ejiri tago-no-ura)

Shore of Tago Bay, Ejiri at Tōkaidō

Men have cast their fishing nets from the prow. All day they pull up nets of emptiness, over and over and over. All this hard work in harsh light, and all they catch is sunburn. They will return home at the end of the day, once again, with nothing to show for their efforts. It is not easy catching the nothingness.

On the shore, workers are tiny and insignificant, raking the flats for salt. Some have already gathered the salt, and now they are carrying their bags to the kilns. Inside the kilns, water boils to keep the salt. These workers will have much to show for their efforts. It is not easy boiling down a day into a single moment.

None of them care that they are close to the Tōkaidō highway. That road could take them far from all of this salt and lack of fish and pull of oars. The road is always there, yet these people always stay performing the same tasks as their ancestors. Small details persisted. The more they struggled, the more they failed, like sunlight, like heartbeats, like salt trying to avoid crystallizing in a kiln, like birds circling uncertain where to land, if to land. It is not easy to be so near a road that can take us elsewhere and stay doing the same meaningless task.

Mount Fuji is always in the background, always with snow on its peak, always below the setting sun. The sense of Always is the only constant we have in this world. Even that is temporary, dissolving like water in the kiln. It is not easy being temporary.

Sun is in a net,
taken to the kiln to bake,
turns to salt in heat.

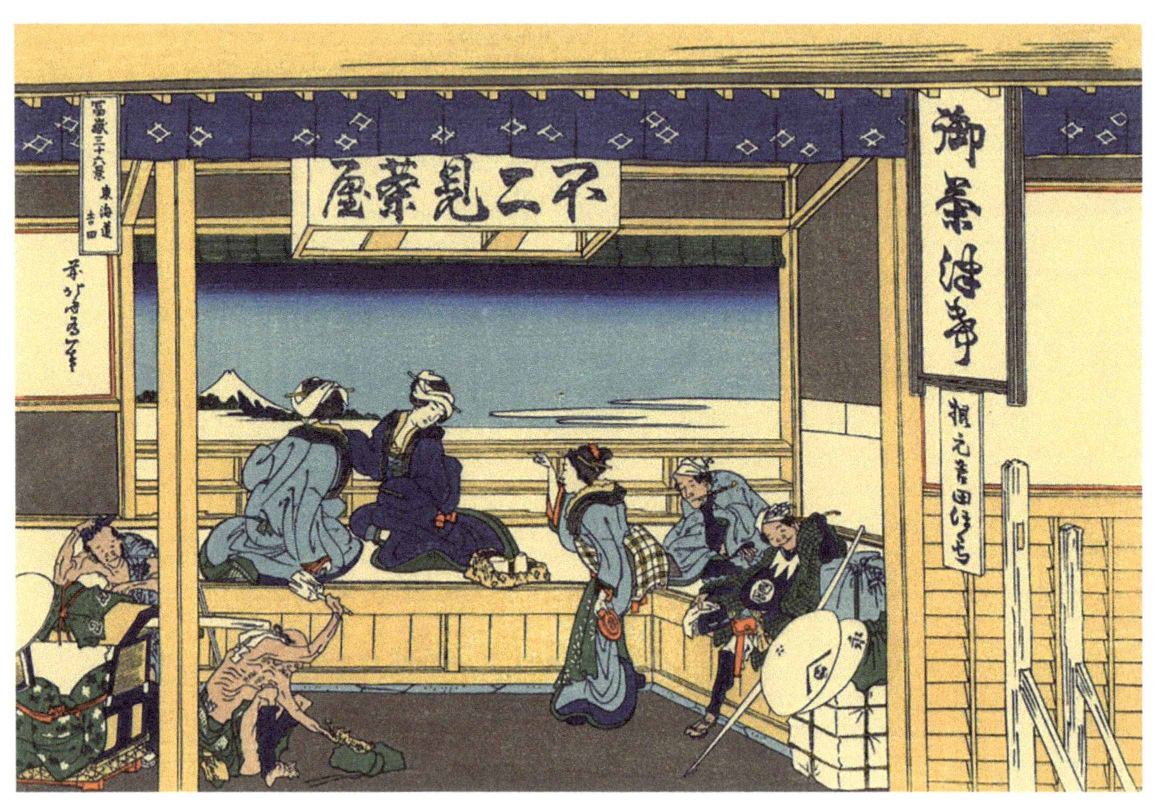

日本語: 東海道吉田 (Tōkaidō Yoshida)

Yoshida at Tōkaidō

At this waystation, on the edge of the Tōkaidō highway, Mount Fuji in the background. Men and women are eating or resting. I cannot afford to eat. I have to feast on the memory of love.

Three women are pointing excitedly at the mountain, but not everyone cares. Still, they point and blush like they have met their first love. The mountain is there, where it has always been; the mountain has not descended into the ocean along with the sun.

A man has a mallet, and he is about to strike whatever is inside his bag. Another man is leaning on a heavy woven yellow chest. Yet another tired man has crossed his right leg over his left leg, and considers if his stack of tied packages is too tall, although they are as light as paper. None of them seem to be thinking about love.

A man with a long pipe offers me a sample of its tobacco smoke smell, but not its taste.

I keep filling my dreams with my wife, building dreams as layers of clouds. I have inhabited my own skin long enough. No one else would want my body except my shadow, and even then, occasionally, my shadow escapes. Look! There goes my shadow, like tobacco smoke from a long clay pipe's tiny round bowl.

Love is folding and unfolding like origami.

When traveling far,
go light as morning's first light;
leave shadow behind.

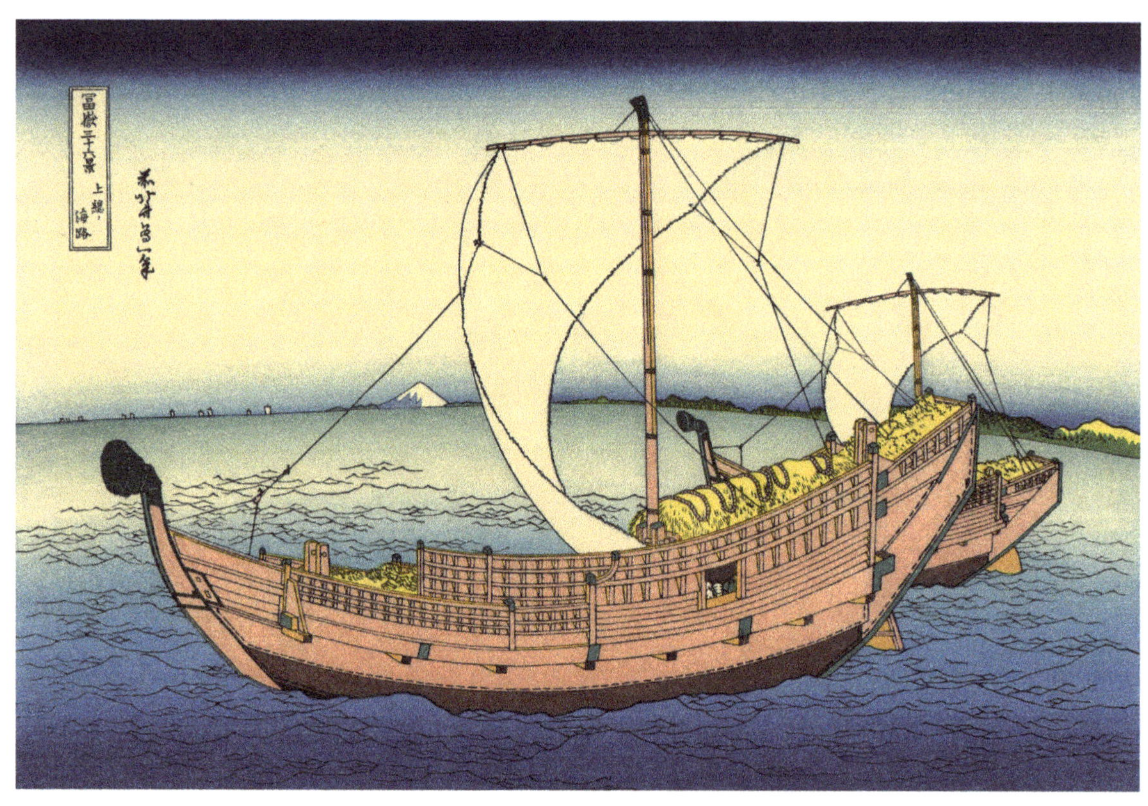

日本語: 上総の海路 (Kazusa no kairo)

The Kazusa Province Sea Route

What is beauty? Is it two junks carrying unknown treasures in treacherous water that finally discover calm water? Nature, seen and not seen. What do you see in the noiseless sea spray or the sails full of helpful wind? Do you see the lives of the trees that were sacrificed to build the ships? I see the beauty in the unfamiliar.

When I was young, I greeted my future wife every day by gasping, *How I wish you would be mine.* I traced the tiny lines of cross-hatching, connecting skin, holding together what is true and believable. Now I am rocking inside a boat instead of in the arms of my lover.

How familiar is the unfamiliar? No matter how often I scanned every inch of my wife, I never seemed to notice every detail. There were so many details and so little time in life. So why am I in a boat when I could be with her?

What is beauty? Some would say my wife is as old as the oldest stone. I say, *She earned every wrinkle, every slow sure step, and every ache.* She creaks as much as this wooden boat. I miss her, and I miss how her hair would flap in wind as loosely as these square sails.

Beauty is not absolute. The idea of beauty changes from man to man, from woman to woman. Each vision of beauty is as different as ocean waves, each as different as a boat caught in the rise and settling of waves, each as different as the amount of wind in these sails or the absence of wind.

I remember those early days: the pitch of our marriage bed and the calmness after.

A boat in ocean
is never the beginning
or middle or end.

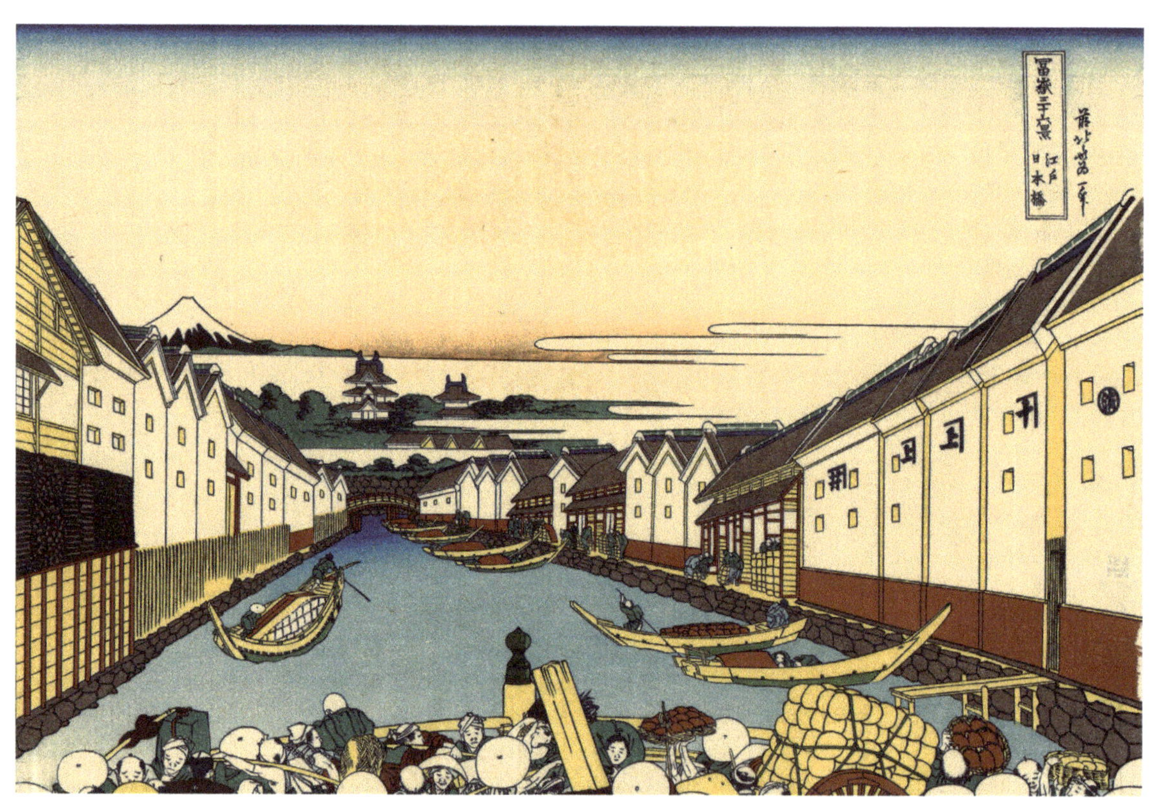

日本語: 江戸日本橋 (Edo Nihon-bashi)

Nihonbashi Bridge in Edo

The Nihonbashi district is a mercantile center with a river dividing the city into *before* and *after*. This wooden bridge holds the two sides from drifting further apart. I have made the mistake of trying to cross in a crowd. No one can move until another person moves. Inching across takes a whole day. I feel as crushed as wheat under a grindstone.

Packages crash into me and never apologize. I find more elbows than there are arms. A cart filled with round packages is held down by netting, but no one pushes or pulls it. Someone holds a tray full of fresh baked buns high in the air to get past my greedy hands. Someone else is carrying some wooden planks. A man stares over the bridge trying to decide if it is easier to walk on water instead of being trapped in the middle of the bridge with nowhere to go.

Three boats pole on the river. The boats have enough room to maneuver. There are other boats tied to walls, and the boats only begin moving when the water laps against the gray wall.

I can see both Mount Fuji and Edo Castle in the distance. They are as near as the moon and sun, and just as far. I cannot move anywhere in this crowd; nor can I get in a boat and sail anywhere. In this crowd, I cannot get closer to my home and wife; but when I am shoved back, I am even further, taking longer, and my longing is trapped with nowhere to go.

I am wearing a large white hat that is hiding my face. I am almost to the center. If I touch the post, will it be real? My feet tell me that I have not moved in hours. Perhaps, I am the bridge, with people walking all over me, aimlessly starting, hesitating, and stopping. Life flows like a backward river.

The bridge never moves—
snails are faster than people,
days go spring to fall.

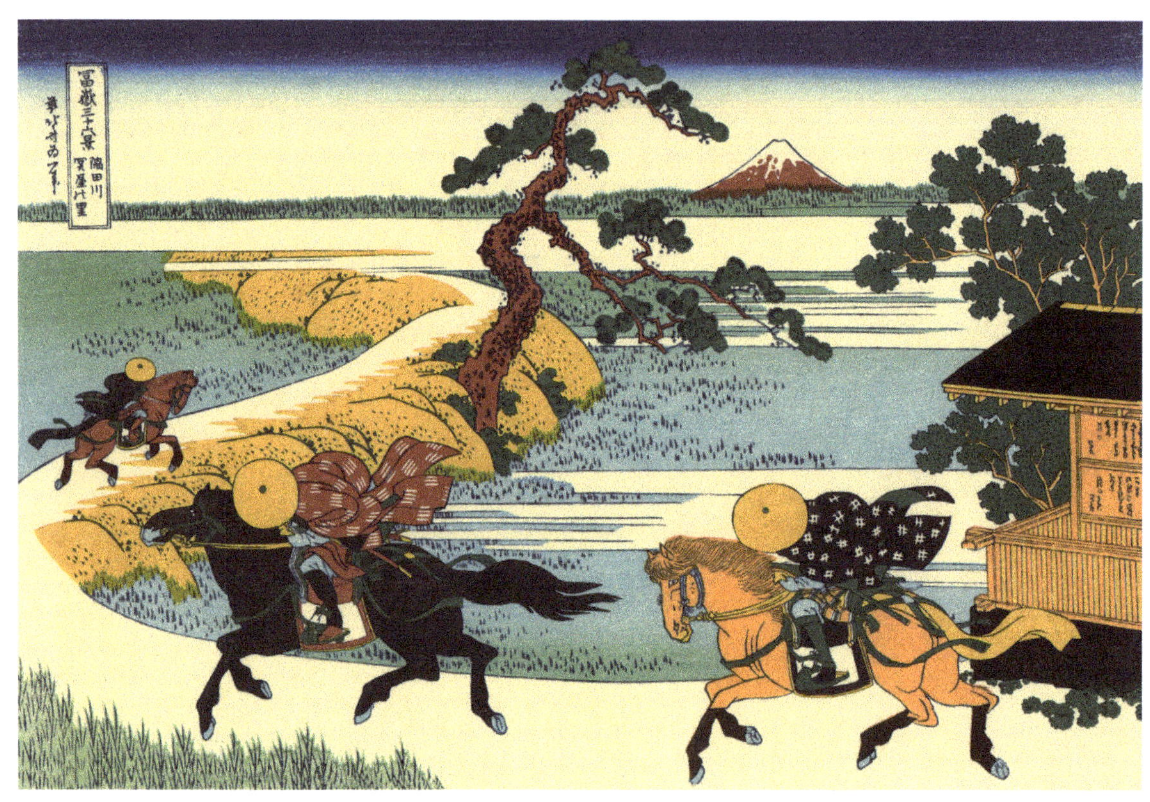

日本語: 隅田川関屋の里 (Sumidagawa Sekiya no sato)

Barrier Town on the Sumida River

Three men riding horses leave wind stirring the world. Their horses' hooves are ripping sounds, in a hurry, faster than color. Two of the riders lean to the left on their saddles to help their speed as they head toward the turn ahead on the right. The rider ahead has already made that right turn and is far ahead. It is dangerous and mysterious to move this fast.

They are trying to deliver mail before the ink on the paper dries. At their pace, words fly off the page.

Movement tells us what we are supposed to be, and when we stop, we forget whatever we knew.

I do not think the world intended to be so fast. It takes me a day just to start to write in a diary. This world is hurrying on a country road, passing the Sekiya village near the Sumida River. Racing does not mean that the world will go any faster. The Emperor must want good news to travel fast.

I write on the surface of the Sumida River. Water will carry my message to Mount Fuji. No horse could outrace time or rivers. Already the mountain is writing back in the clouds above her.

Mount Fuji's dispatch finds its way into my heart like a cricket sound.

A horse's mane flows—
a black flood, fast as my love.
Orchids are her eyes.

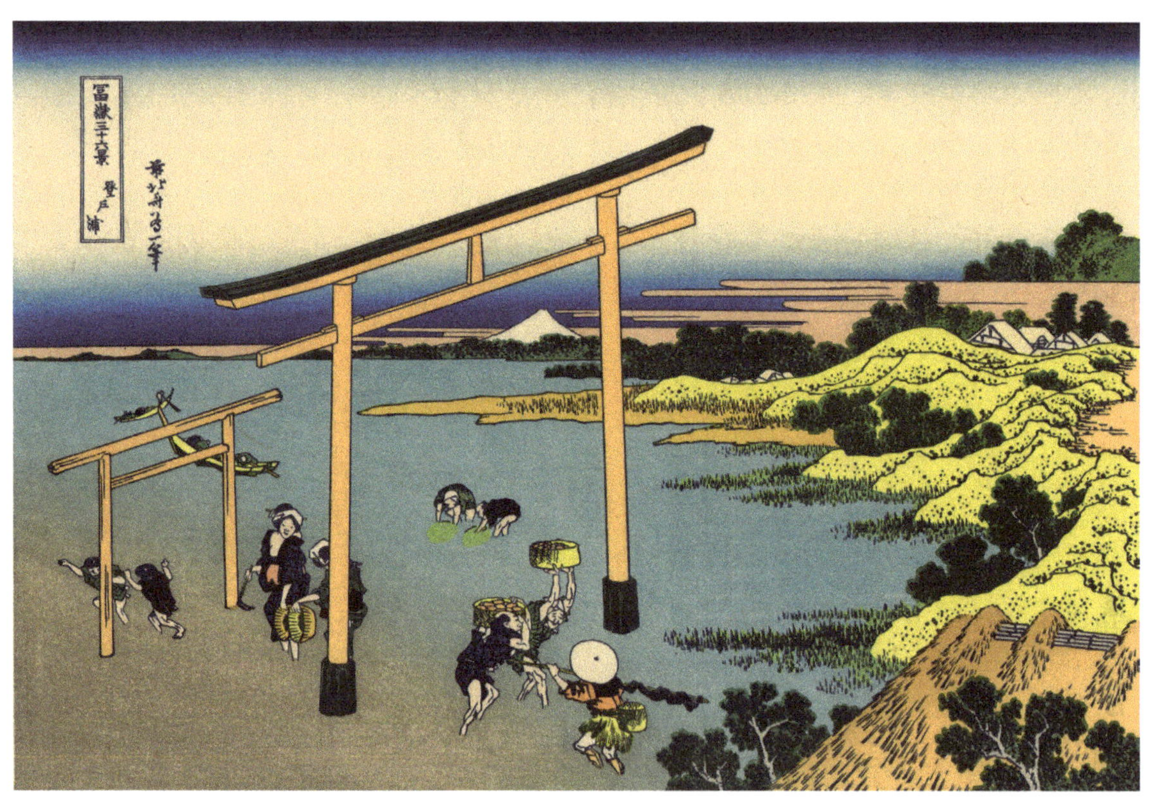

日本語: 登戸浦 (Noboto-ura)

Bay of Noboto

People are pursuing shellfish on the Noboto-ura bay in Shimosa province. The turning water keeps the crabs out of reach. Crawfish are as fast and elusive as love or life. People reach into the water, but water distorts where their prey is now. Sometimes people catch enough crawfish for their basket to take to market. Too often the baskets are empty.

Two small boys are playing on the edge of the water. I hear an adult scolding the children. Children will do what interests them, and what they want to do is not work. Too often a child will do what a child will do and an adult will scold those childish ways.

I want to join the boys. I want to make up rules of a game as I play. I want to feel the cool water on my toes. How foolish it was when I became an adult. Someone would tell me to act my age, but how do others of my age act? How many men would rather run and play as a child? Who wants responsibility when the earth provides what we need? I want to play so hard that my shadow never catches up to me.

Mount Fuji laughs at everyone's efforts, and its laughter is seagulls. This contagious laugh wrinkles the land permanently. It awakens this small village and opens the house doors like surprised mouths. It wakes the hermit crab from its shell. It wakes me from a nap.

In my lap is an offering of a tiny sand crab.

Trying to catch stars
or crabs is difficult work—
dreams are easier.

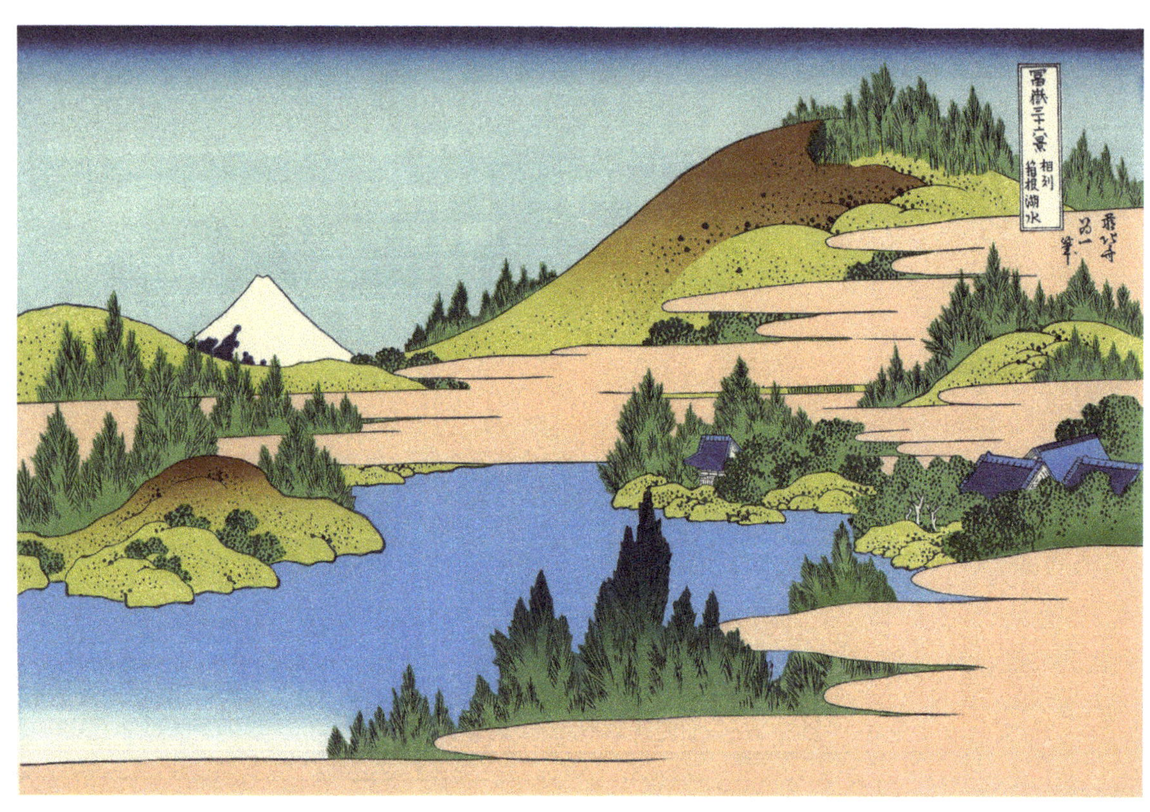

日本語: 相州箱根湖水 (Sōshū Hakone kosui)

The Lake of Hakone in Sagami Province

I approach a minor village near an insignificant lake adjacent to clumps of pine. Pine needles tinkle like wind chimes in the slightest wind. In the distance, a window creaks open to let in fresh air. Behind the houses are sandy spaces all the way toward a long hill. At this angle, I can see Mount Fuji peeking, wearing a white cone hat. The lake is tiny. It does not reflect any images on it.

I could meditate here, shallow breaths, and let the air surround me like a lover's arms. Will this area accept a stranger? Or will the villagers insist I move on, taking my old bones to somewhere else?

A rich man can hire others to carry his heavy loads, but I have to carry as little as possible and dispose of anything I do not need. I can count all my possessions on one hand, and it is the same number of houses in this area. But the one thing I carry with me is love. Yesterday, I discarded my cough. I had carried it too far, and its weight was slowing me down.

I found a new walking stick that had fallen from a diseased tree. I accepted this gift. It will help me struggle from place to place. Mount Fuji is kind to foolish old men. Perhaps because it understands love.

I promised the mountain I would spend more time with my wife when I get home. This was an easy promise, one I am least likely to break. This walking stick will help me get home faster.

A stout branch for a crutch is better than a thin branch when I have a feeble limp.

I hear the branch in my hand each time it touches the ground, saying, *This is not home. Home is what you think about all of the time when you are not daydreaming.*

Wind in pines makes sounds—
my wife is turning in sleep,
hugging her dreams tight.

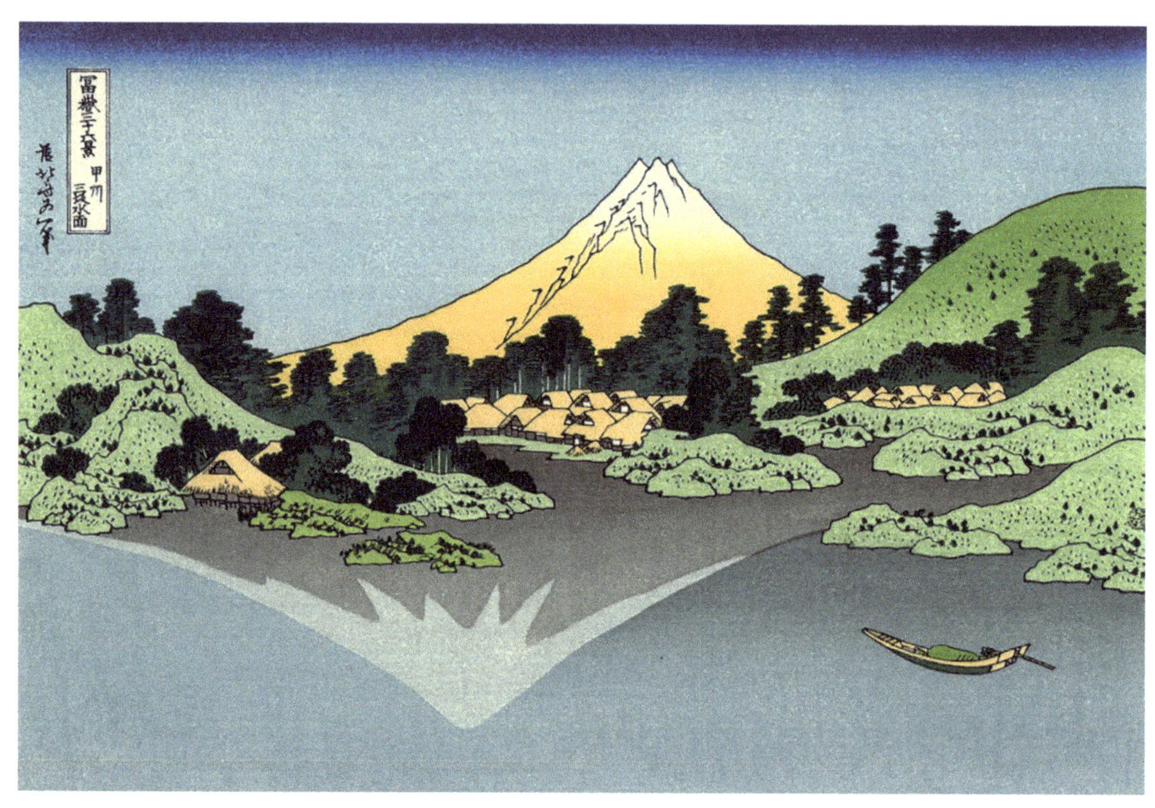

日本語: 甲州三坂水面 (Kōshū Misaka suimen)

Mount Fuji Reflects in Lake Kawaguchi, Seen from the Misaka Pass in Kai Province

A boat returning does not dare to disturb Mount Fuji's image. No birds in the sky, no clouds, no tree lines mirror in the lake. No one ripples the mountain in the lake. No words appear in my poetry. Whatever I sketch vanishes. The wind sketches this reminder, *Pay attention, pay attention, pay attention.*

The lake is a compass telling me that the center of my attention should not be on the lake—it should always be on the mountain, always the echo of the mountain; only Mount Fuji matters. The reflection is saying, *Pay attention, pay attention, pay attention.*

My mind looks for all the images that vanished. Perhaps they went to visit my wife, far away. Maybe we are all reflections on water. Only Mount Fuji remains important. *Pay attention, pay attention, pay attention.*

I think I am on the pass in Kai Province. A lonely sound without a reflection. Every moment disturbs me. I have trouble focusing on Mount Fuji. Look at my sketches. I want to tear them up into clouds. Mount Fuji echoes, *Pay attention, pay attention, pay attention.*

Only Mount Fuji can find our eyes no matter where we stand. Boats come near, empty. Houses hide from the mountain in the dark shadows of trees. A bell could echo until it reaches the mountain's mirror image, and the bell's sound would be swallowed. The bell could remind me, *Pay attention, pay attention, pay attention.*

I can almost see my wife coming out of our thatched-roof house, recalling how I once filled her arms. *Pay attention, pay attention, pay attention.*

The mountain devours images. The mountain is dancing. Water teaches deception, all of this un-realness. I can't pay attention. Silence devours silence.

Fuji drowns in lake;
emptiness is a cast boat
sent to save nothing.

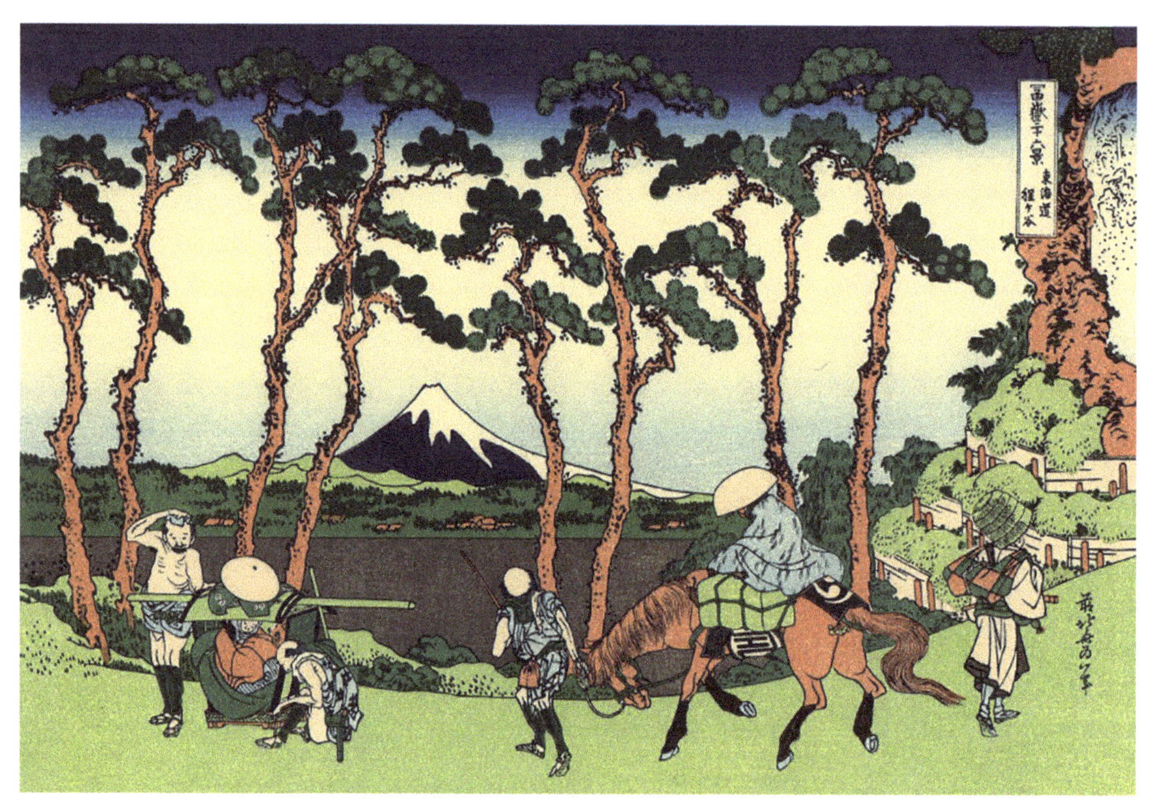

日本語: 東海道程ケ谷 (Tōkaidō Hodogaya)

Hodogaya on the Tōkaidō

I have traveled this far to get this lost. I feel that I have finally left the large city of Edo behind me, and its memory is merely dust left behind my shoes. Now I am following my wife's voice toward love, an echo left in a conch shell, a sea breeze finding one bell no one has rung, light traveling through the maze of leaf veins. I have not traveled far enough. I still have more of my journey left. Now I am not sure where I am. Someone tells me.

At Hodogaya, the road has pine trees on both sides. Mount Fuji is always on my side. I never feel that I am getting anywhere. The mountain never moves, and I journey without advancing. I have witnessed the same blade of grass for five days. I am not the only one that feels that they are as immobile as the mountain. Although I am guided by my urge to go home, time goes nowhere.

There is a rider that has fallen asleep, bent over, his hat covering his face with shade. He has a guide tugging the horse reins. The horse has had one foot up, ready for motion, frozen in place. The ground moves, but the horse never seems to move. If the rider wakes, a season will have passed, and we will all still be here on this same road, near the same pine, with the same mountain, where we all have always been waiting. We are lost in time. How far do we have to go to still be here?

We are not getting where we are going in this standstill landscape.

There are two men carrying a long pole with a woven traveling basket in the middle. Inside the basket is a woman, impatient with the lack of movement. She comments that she has grown older since she arrived here. One of the men is scratching his head trying to puzzle out this mystery. He is expected to carry, and not to question, so when he scratches his head, all he finds is lice. The other man bends down trying to fix what he cannot fix. Time refuses to move.

The faraway is never nearer. The distance we have traveled is being undone.

Crocuses open
whenever they feel ready—
coaxing does not work.

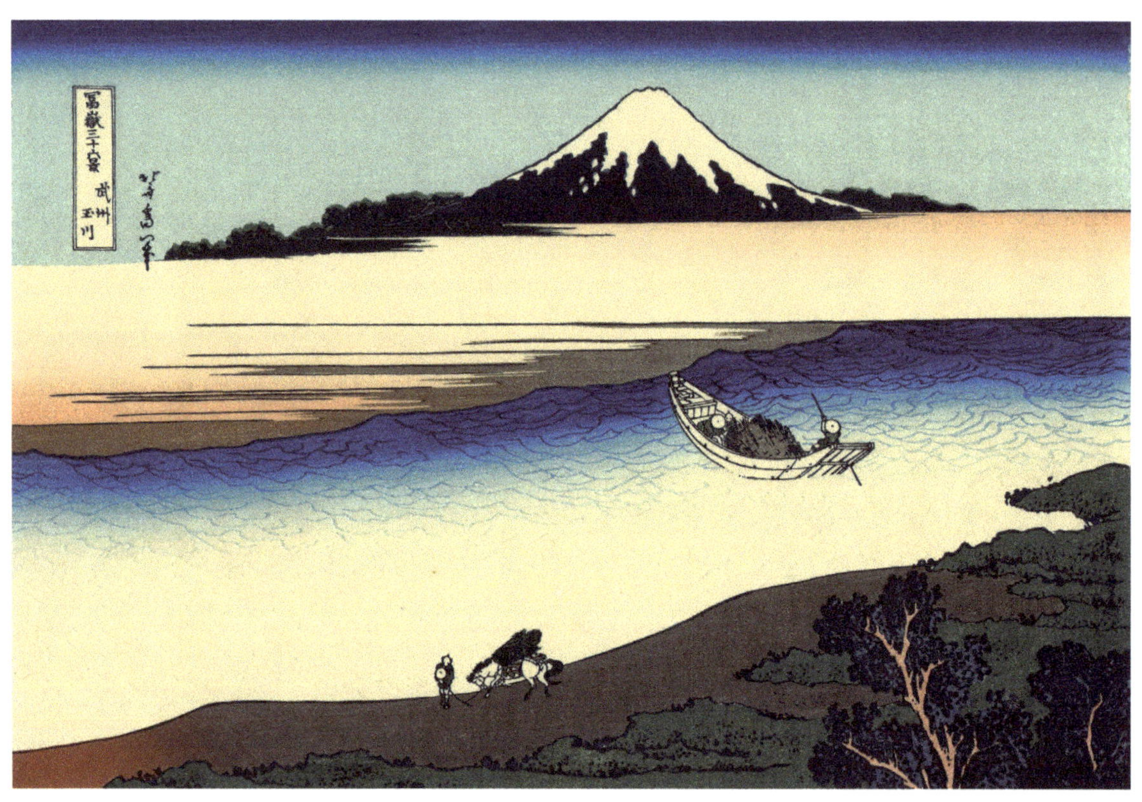

日本語: 武州玉川 (Bushū Tamagawa)

Tama River in Musashi Province

I am on a large rise looking down at the river. My eyes will go further than my voice. In this height, clouds catch in my white beard. If I were to go home now, my wife would have to dry the moisture on my eyebrows. She would ask why my forehead is tan with blush. I would have to admit that I have been dreaming that the mountain goddess and her had merged into one spirit. She would choke laughter and warn that I was still a lusty man regardless of my age or ability. The more I imagine, the more my body is a river never finding home.

Down below this hill, a man has guided his hot, tired horse to the water. The horse is drinking the memory of journeys. The man is holding either a hat or a shield. Is there a difference between hat and shield when the world is at peace? He seems to be the only person moving away from Mount Fuji.

There is a boat in the river, and I see two men with a bundle between them. From here, the pile appears to be stacked pieces of wood. There are no trees to cut on either side, so I cannot be correct. Their boat is pointed to Mount Fuji, but the boat is sitting in the middle of the river, not moving, and neither man is fishing.

I wonder what my wife is doing now. Is she looking for a stick to toss on the fire? Is she chuckling at my odd challenge of painting at my age? On this hill, I lose all perspective.

Everything looks down from here.

When you are seventy, both you and a wooden boat creak.

Frogs in trees singing,
below the water is stilled.
Reeds repeat the songs.

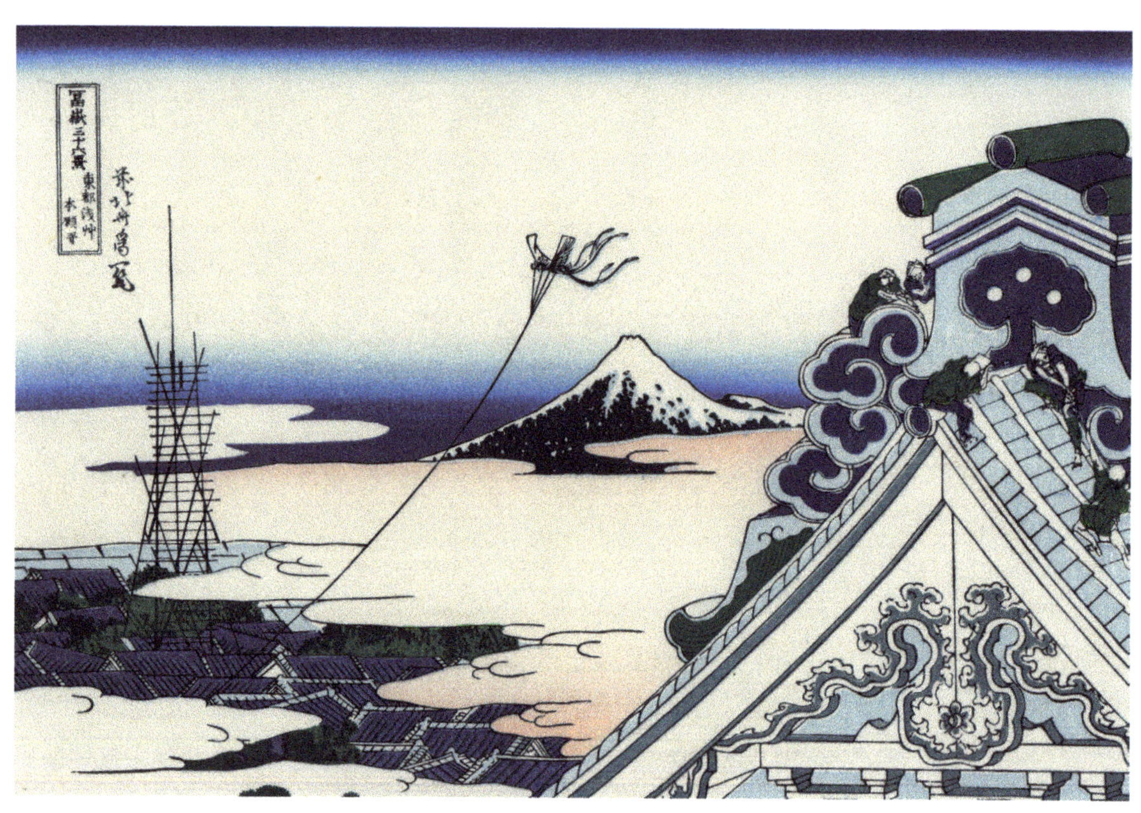

日本語: 東都浅草本願寺 (Tōto Asakusa honganji)

Asakusa Hongan-ji Temple in the Eastern Capital

It is said that if you touch the door of this temple, evil transforms. I am not entering.

I glance toward the roof to see Mount Fuji behind the temple. Someone is flying a kite, and the clouds nudge the kite away. So much is happening; little is transpiring.

One of the temple followers has a painted image of Amida Buddha tied to his fingers. He is on his way to trying to break the continuous circle of life. He wants to transform the errors he has made in life before he dies. His life is this string, this picture of the Buddha, his prayer to fly all evil away.

I am not leaving.

Most cannot hope to escape the cycle of birth and death and love. We have no power over the distance between living and dying and love between. It is as impractical as controlling a kite once the wind has it.

Both the picture of the Buddha and the kite are on a string, and a string can be easily untied as tied. I am the kind of person who tugs at strings just to see what happens next.

Someday, by testing and pestering at my own string, I will unravel, accidentally, the one string that holds my life together. Will love be the only thing that remains? Please, let it be always love.

String knots and unknots,
threads separate into one,
all clinging loosens.

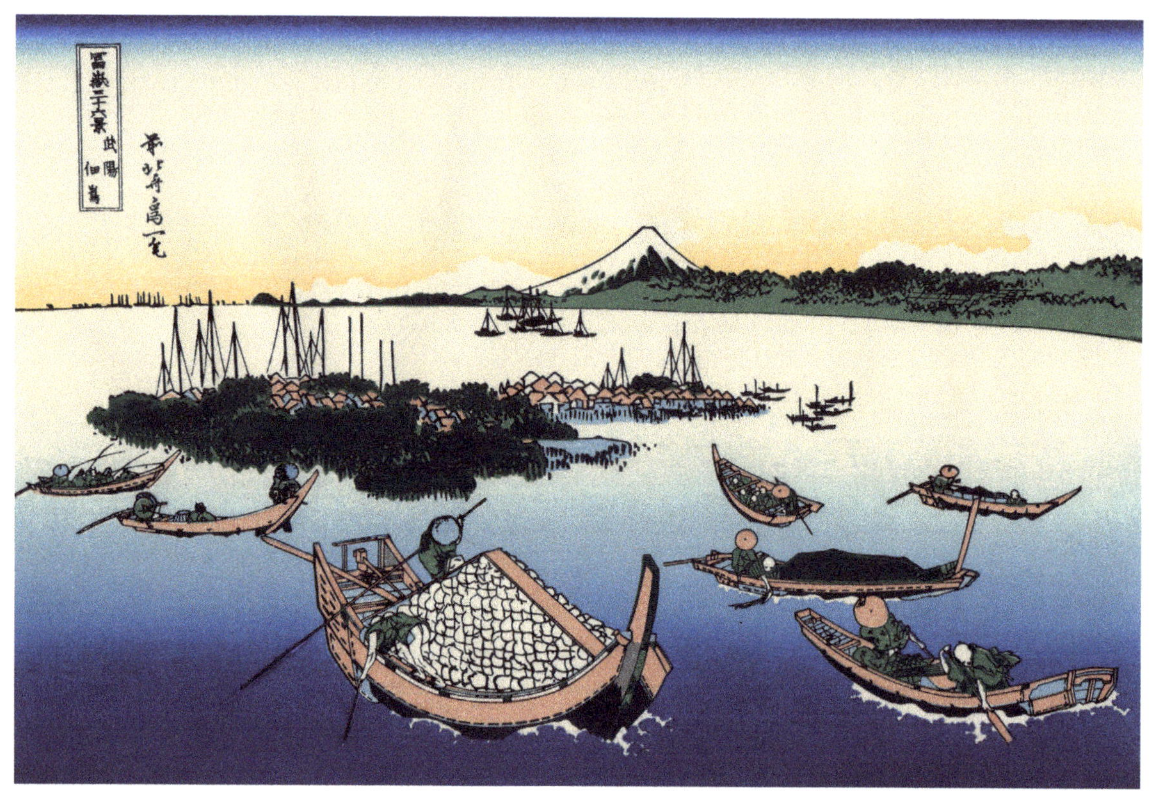

日本語: 武陽佃島 (Buyō Tsukuda-jima)

Tsukuda Island in Musashi Province

Evening is approaching with sails from the far horizon heading to this port. All fishermen and transport boats are pushing their long poles to get here. Some ships tied to the docks near the village sell fish fresh from baskets.

The water is meditating. Beyond the grassy shores and trees, further than the hills, Mount Fuji is watching and counting the sails flapping like kimonos billowing in winds.

The boat closest to mine is a transport. It is laden with goods I cannot afford. The man who pushes the boat using a pole has no time to talk to a lowly person like me. The quick plops of a pole in water speaks to his restlessness of getting in before dark. He refuses to admit, once again, that he has forgotten a lantern.

I have reconciled with the water. I promise not to drink the water if it promises not to drown me. I have to be careful; all promises have ending dates. I cannot see the bottom of the water, and the water cannot see the bottom of my heart.

The ferryman poles toward the shoreline. It is still a great distance away. Measure for measure, we inch closer. Can the pole feel my anxiety or excitement?

Hurry, pole, hurry; this water is one of the elements, and I do not want to join it just yet. When I am floating in this familiar terror, I know that I am still alive. Is dread a part of enlightenment?

A feather sinking
still has time to save itself.
A duck swims away.

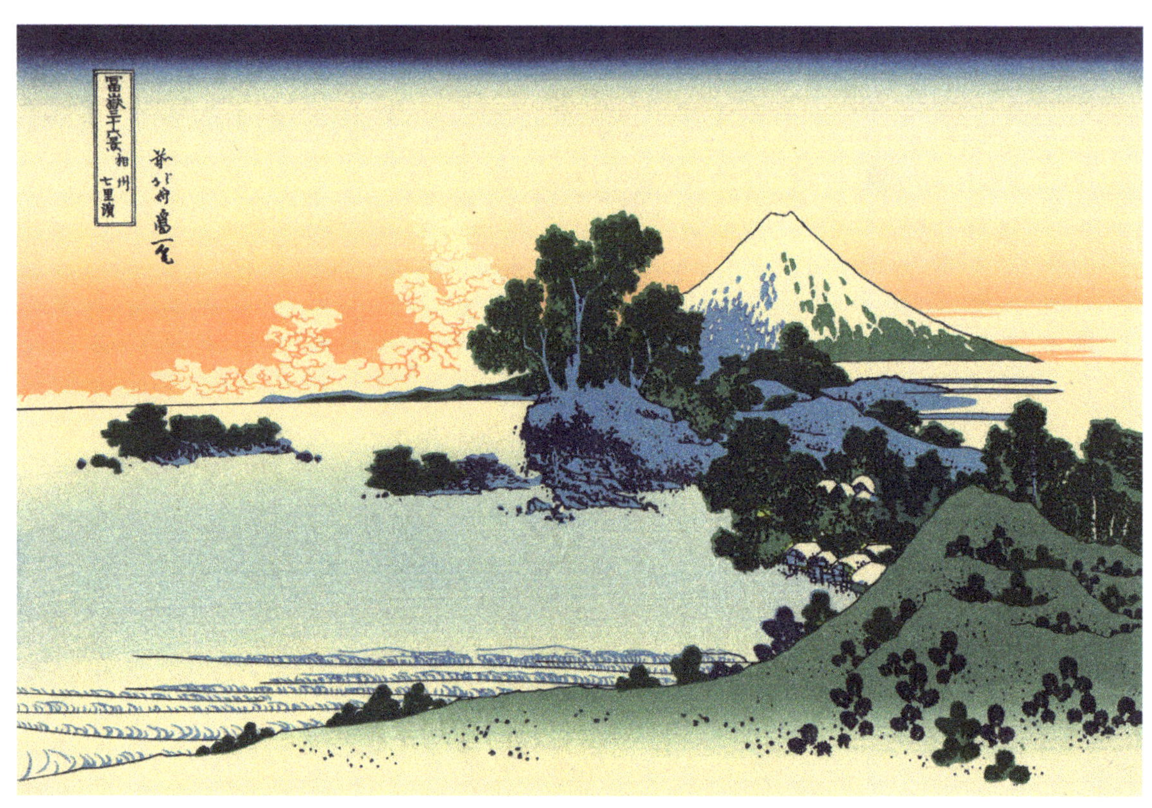

日本語: 相州七里浜 (Soshū Shichiri-ga-hama)

Shichiri Beach in Sagami Province

The coastline curls like my wife's flirting smile.

If people were here, I would have to paint as if they were not on the *Seven-League Beach*. I already had to move to another location so I would not focus on the sand dunes and cactus. What distracts does not belong. My wife paints her way into my heart.

I want to see Mount Fuji without those tall trees blocking my view. Every object needs to move so I can see the mountain. Distractions take our eyes away from what we need to notice and focus on what we should ignore.

Why did I take this journey when I could have been home with my wife?

At the bend, the houses of Koshigoe have thatched roofs. I can tell the difference of poverty by that straw covering. I am too poor to live in such poverty. An open sky night is even too expensive for me.

What I cannot afford distracts me.

There is the pilgrimage site of the island, Enoshima—far left, sitting on the ocean. Summer is coming soon. Clouds pile upon clouds upon clouds crossing over the horizon. My wife enters a cloud. I am distracted.

Everything reminds me I belong elsewhere.

A beach without men—
all my footprints are washed away.
Only waves remain.

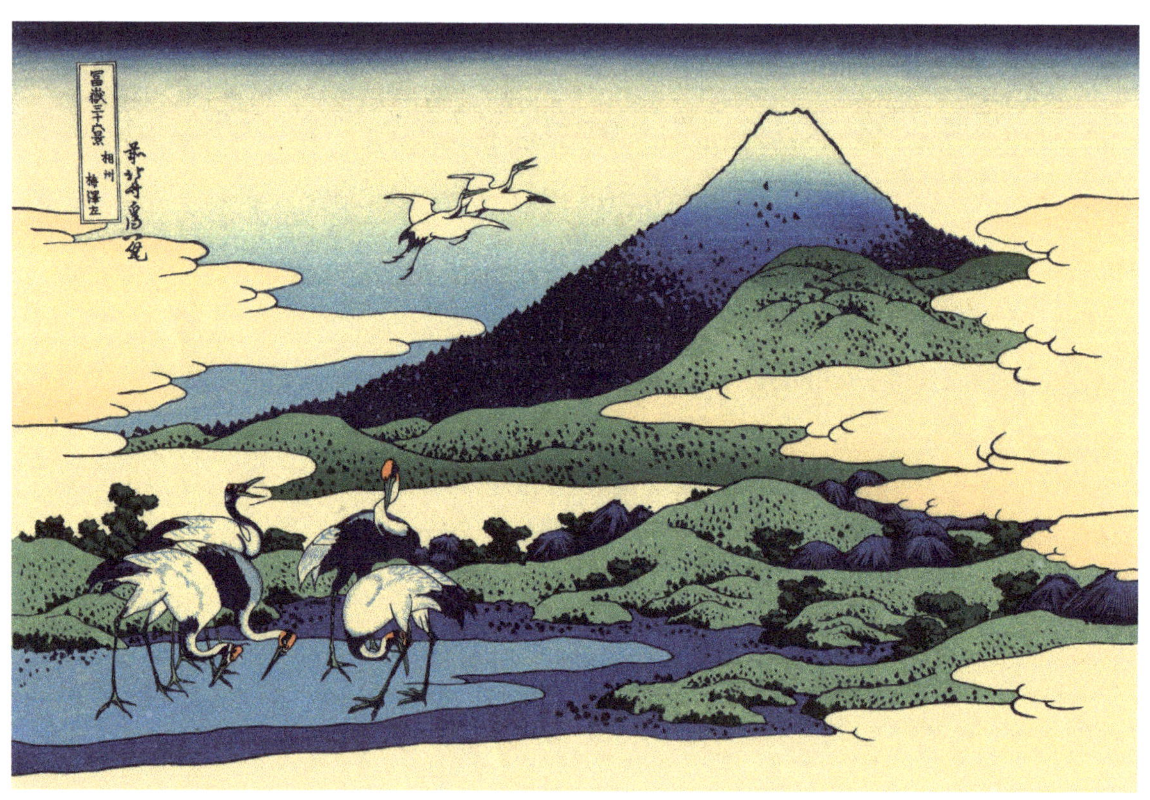

日本語: 相州梅沢庄 (Soshū umezawanoshō)

Umezawa in Sagami Province

Mount Fuji is as tranquil as this stream below. What do I know of silence? The stream takes away all noise and my words. Cranes have taken refuge in foothills in order to escape humans trampling on their sense of peace.

Five cranes are feeding from the stream, eating the silence. Two other cranes try to find the top of Mount Fuji, knowing there is more silence to be found there. How much quietness does anyone need? *More*, the cranes beg, *More*. The mountain provides.

The mountain's imposing cone is deep blue at the base of the mountain and the mountain fades to light blue and white at the summit, rising above the green slopes. My eyes cannot speak as they find the top of Mount Fuji, where everything will vanish into stillness. Bands of pink-tinted clouds cover parts of sky with veils.

Cranes know this is where words do not belong. When I never know what to say, I try to find some words. Words destroy the temporary moment for everyone.

Cranes always know where to find translucent light, and they nest unobtrusively while practicing being a part of soundlessness.

What do I know of meditation? What do I know of silence?

Wind whispers softly;
too much noise for the mountain,
waking from its nap.

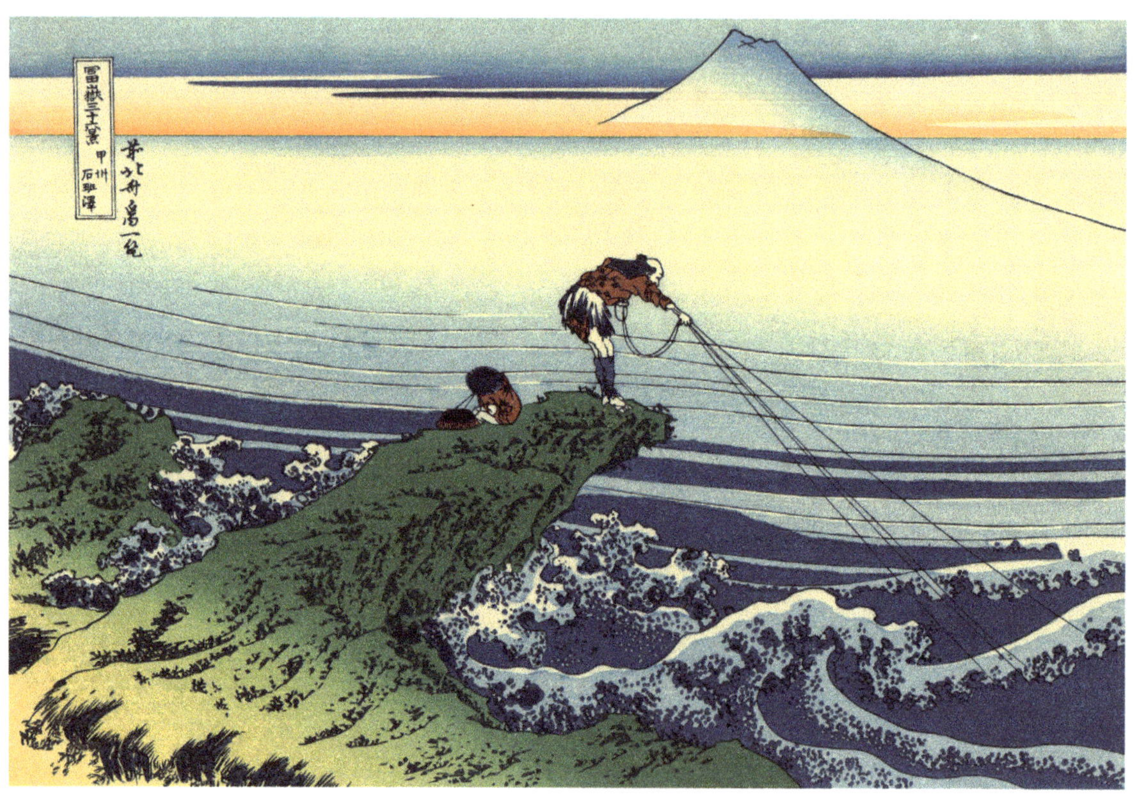

日本語: 甲州石班沢 (Kōshū Kajikazawa)

Kajikazawa in Kai Province

The river swells from snowmelt. Waves toss against the shoreline, a childish temper tantrum. A fisherman and a child are standing on a moss-covered rock. The man is casting his net into the swollen river. Is he trying to capture Mount Fuji's image in his net? His son is playing with small rocks.

Someone will say the boy will never learn how to fish that way. Someone will say the boy must be as industrious as this father who made the net and tosses it into the ocean daily in order to sell fish at the marketplace. But the boy wants to play.

I prefer the habits of a child exploring childish discoveries.

Someday the child will grow out of this wonder. He will tack the net the same way his father, and his father's father, and generations of fishermen stringing nets. He will toss his own net into the ocean from the same moss-covered rock, hoping to find the net filled with fish, then carry his fish back to the same marketplace. He will hope someone will buy his fish. His entire life will depend on luck, skill, and fish. He will want what he cannot get.

For now the boy is lifting rocks, finding bugs underneath. The bugs squirm, and the boy is pleased. His father is screaming and cursing at the waves, the lack of any fish, the storm stirring the waves, the breeze in his hair, the way the world always brings misery. He wants it to end. He casts his line of disappointment. He receives what he expects. He cannot reconcile his life.

The boy never hears his father over the gale. Bugs scatter in all directions, fleeing the wind.

Fish swim in my eyes.
My net wants to capture wind.
I catch loss instead.

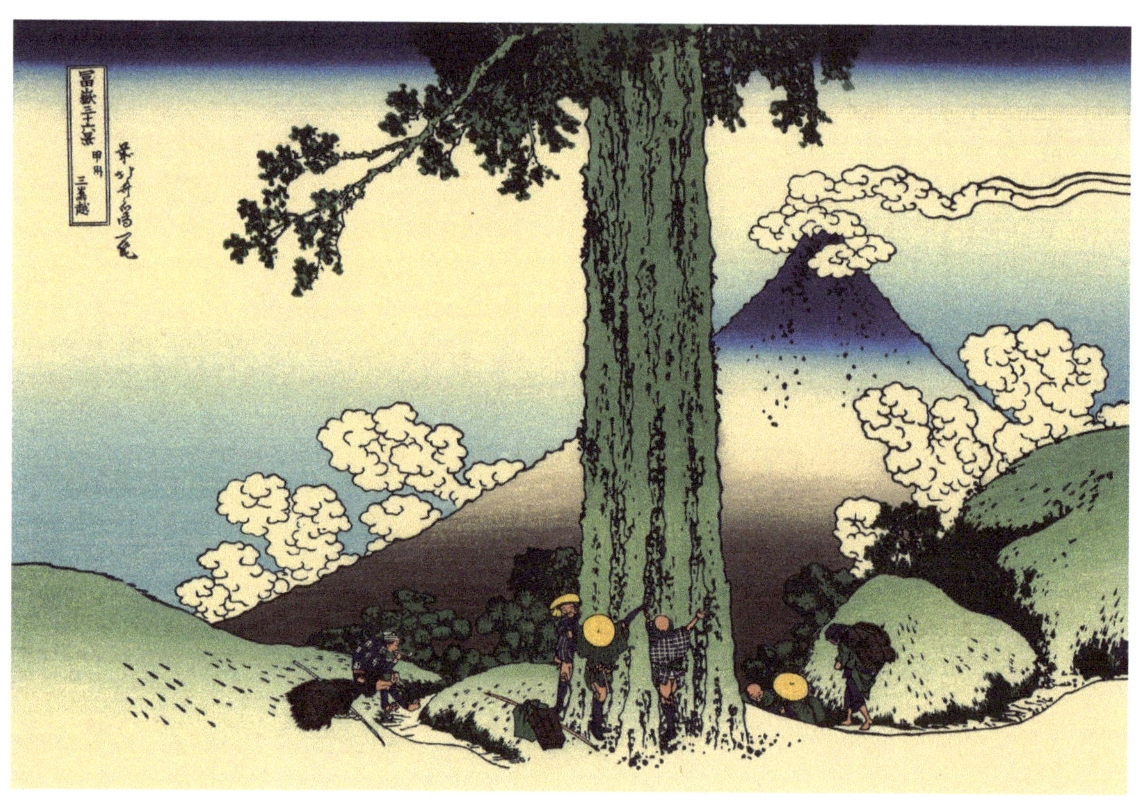

日本語: 甲州三嶌越 (Kōshū Mishima-goe)

Mishima Pass in Kai Province

Kasagumo is an "umbrella cloud," considered to be wandering human deceased spirits.

A long, snaking, snarling, Kasagumo cloud encircles Mount Fuji. Among the unhappy spirits in that cloud is my grandfather, who demands that I mention his name with respect. It is not my fault that I have a faulty memory, probably from years of sake and aimless wanderings. How large is my error? Memory opens and closes like an umbrella. As if to answer, three men try to measure the circumference of the enormous cedar, using their arms extended and fingers touching to determine its size. They fail to determine the answer. How can we measure beauty or nature? Memory cannot stretch that far.

A peasant relaxes, sitting in the shade on a small hill. He is smoking a clay pipe. The smoke from his pipe might be the same as the clouds circling the summit; but one is holy, untouchable, and reverent, while the other includes my ancestor. My grandfather pokes at my memory.

From this viewpoint, that cedar is larger than Mount Fuji. All perspective is illusion. This world will never last long enough to measure, and we will never be able to see through the Kasagumo clouds. The man smoking the pipe might believe the tree is larger than Mount Fuji, but when I hold my hand in front of my eyes, my hand is bigger than the mountain and tree. Size is irrelevant. We live such short lives compared with nature. We are here today in this temporary moment, and we are gone tomorrow with the travelers starting their descent down the northwest side of the Tökaidö Highway. Memory is those footsteps heading away. The cedar branches are tangled in a weaving of light, leaves, and wind.

We are just traveling through life regardless if we are standing still. These light-green clouds of ancestors try to tell us that same message. Sweat on my forehead lasts longer than the message.

When I get home, I will try to measure my wife's love.

Ancestors! Tell me—
does a flower perfume last
as long as petals?

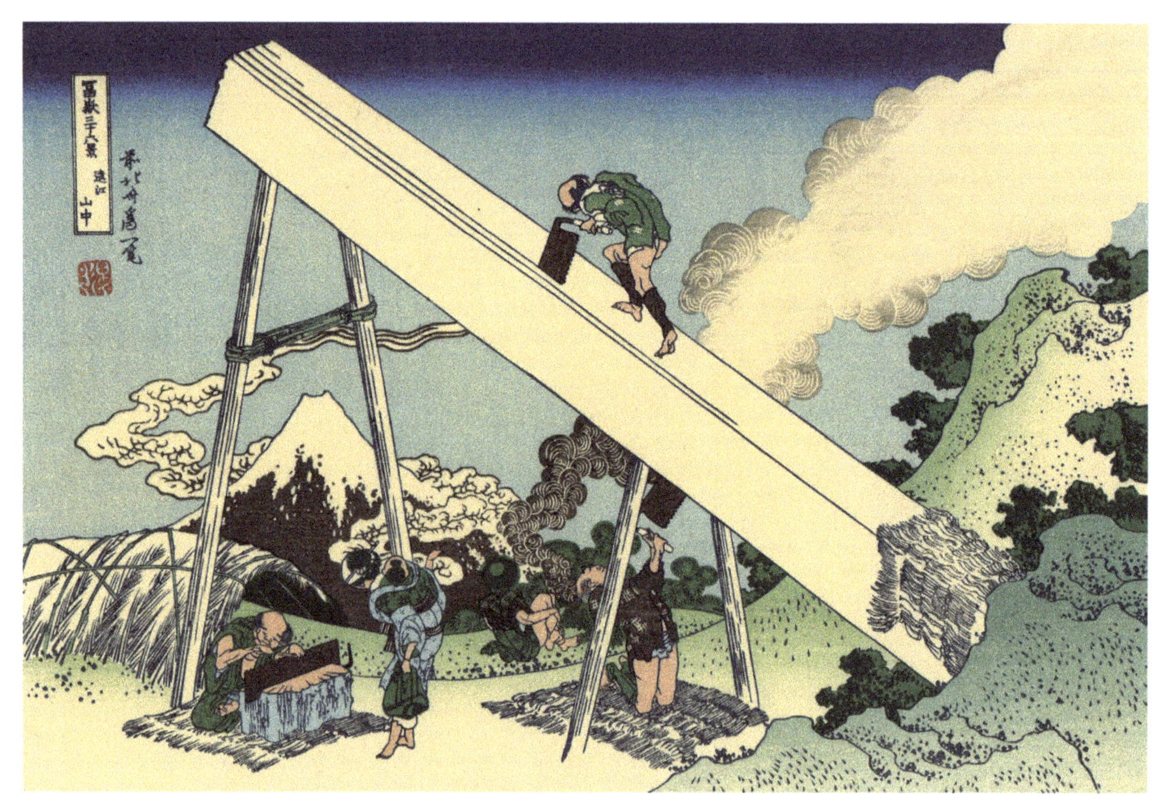

日本語: 遠江山中 (Tōtōmi sanchū)

Mount Fuji from the Mountains of Tōtōmi

Lumbermen are working on a huge log in the Totomi mountains. One man is standing on a long pillar as he cuts straight down. He is splitting boards, shaping the lumber. He has been performing this work for thousands of years.

What in this world remains? Mount Fuji, misery, rain, heat, rocks, water, snow, and clouds.

We are puffs of air. We begin dying as soon as we are born. We are born into this world begging for air, and we exit this world begging for air. The earth was here before any of us were born, and this world will be here long after we are gone. We were born to be temporary, but the earth will be here forever. What do I know of suffering?

I see the tree cut, and it is suffering. We are bending nature to our will by building roads and houses, but nature tries to bend us to its will by changing weather. It was hot and it snowed yesterday.

Men have been working hard for centuries, the same way as their ancestors, in the same job trained by watching their ancestors. Not one slight change. Some of us are born to be carpenters, some fishermen, some shipbuilders, and some will become samurai.

I remember the senselessness of the waterwheel. How it poured out water not caring if anyone placed a bucket to catch the water. What do I know about suffering? I am less than spilled water.

Ants build a small mound,
removing dirt—uncertain—
rain, or no more rain.

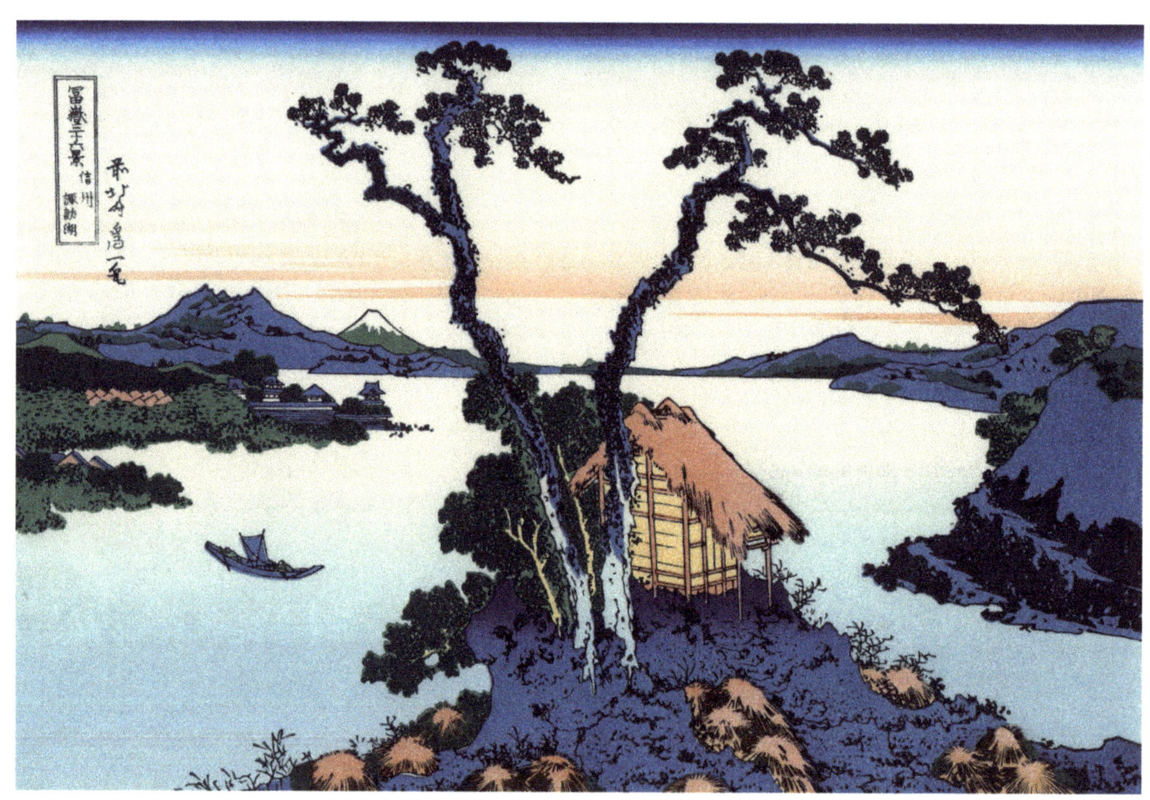

日本語: 信州諏訪湖 (Shinshū Suwa-ko)

Lake Suwa in Shinano Province

There is a natural hot spring under the surface of the lake. When the lake freezes, the lower parts of water are still circulating, making knee-high ice pressure ridges. The gods caused those ridges while crossing the lake. The guardian god had to leave his sanctuary to meet his wife, the goddess, on the opposite bank.

All men should return to their wives with that same intense need. We seldom do. I have been absent too long. I began with a spiritual search and brought paper to illustrate what I see. However, I kept thinking about my wife, how I miss her, how I have to slow down to enjoy her presence. At first, I thought I was crying softly, but it is the slow rain coming in through the straw roof of this shack. I am nearing my wife. My shadow can almost touch her shadow.

Invited to stay at this small shack, I remarked that this could easily be a shrine. Although it is so insignificant, as small as an afterthought, I shall honor this humble building in my painting. The rain was half-asleep.

There are two large trees behind this brown hut, two fingers testing the direction of the wind. It is far from Mount Fuji. Rain is coming in faster, skimming the lake with its music. The redden morning sky is graying. The water in the distance is changing into a lighter blue, holding the sun's reflection. A boat has sailed out to rescue the sun from drowning.

Almost home is not close enough. My wife is waiting.

A roof, a slow leak,
red morning untouched by rain—
what else do I need?

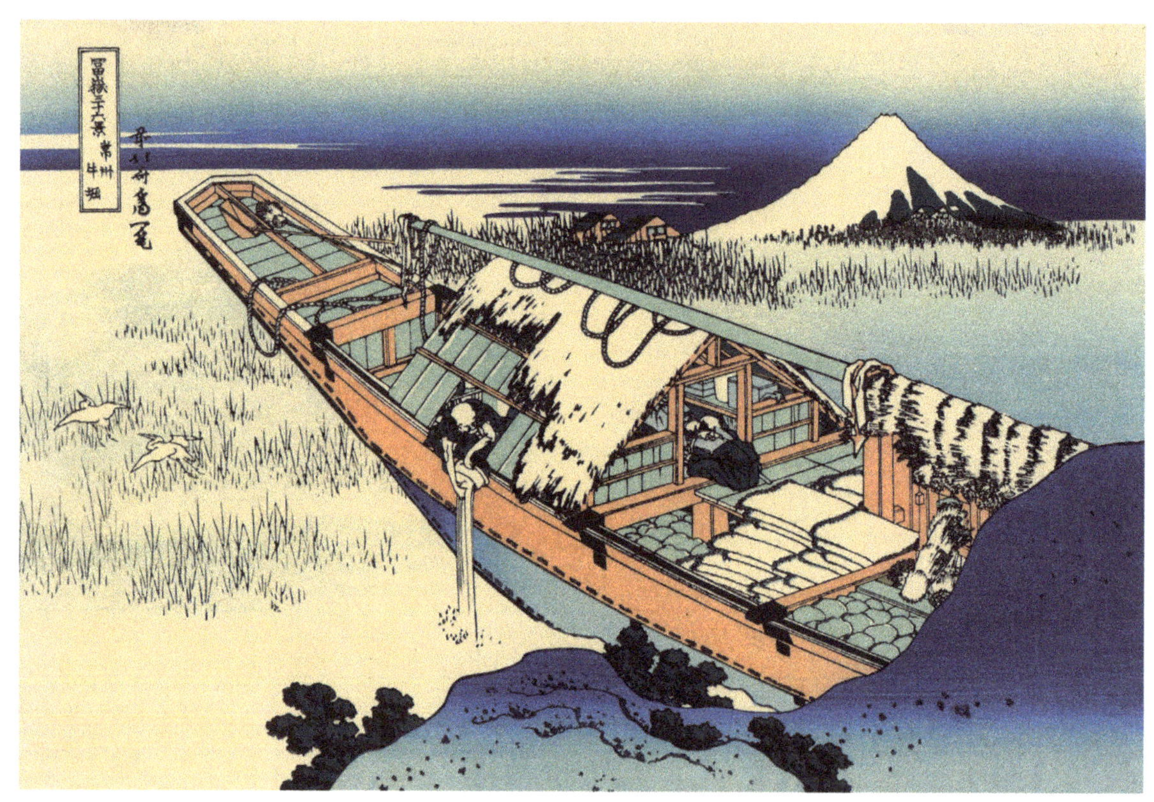

日本語: 常州牛掘 (Jōshū Ushibori)

Ushibori in Hitachi Province

This inland harbor connects to Chöshi. A boat with a kaya grass roof has anchored in the marshy water. Its bow rises diagonally to the left. A dune conceals its stern.

The boatman is washing rice for his dinner. He leans against the gunwale, tossing out the rinse water, disturbing the nearby cranes into flight.

He shows me his cargo. Sacks and reed mats are stowed in an orderly pile. On a cabin shelf are his books and ledgers. According to the numbers, he is prosperous. I conclude I do not need a ledger to keep track of my poverty.

However, my life has been rich. I have been with my wife for about fifty years. I still appreciate her, even when I am away—especially, when I have been away for too long. I can count the stars and the fleas as part of my riches. I can count every one of my wrinkles, and I have earned each of them.

I have asked myself along the way, *What do I know about silence?* The answer is Mount Fuji. It is now in my heart, eyes, and hands. When I paint these images, I cannot speak, for I am intense within the moment. When I remember the roads, the cliffs, the cluster of trees, the people I have met along the trail, no one can take away my speechless feelings. Mount Fuji has moved with me, yet it never moved.

The boatman showed me numbers that were meaningless to me. The workers showed me the meaninglessness of repetition. Children showed me that the best appreciation of nature and time is to enjoy each moment as it happens. Now I will play with colors and paint. Today I am a toddler with a toddler's surprised eyes. Fuji is a spinning top!

A horse; a spider.
a marble; a hat; a snail.
A child plays with rocks.

About the Author

Martin Willitts Jr. is a Quaker. He is a retired librarian and musician living in Syracuse, New York. He is an editor for *The Comstock Review* and a judge for the New York State Fair Poetry Contest. He has been nominated for seventeen Pushcart and thirteen Best of the Net awards. Winner of the 2012 Big River Poetry Review's William K. Hathaway Award; 2013 Bill Holm Witness Poetry Contest; 2013 "Trees" Poetry Contest; 2014 Broadsided Award; 2014 Dylan Thomas International Poetry Contest; *Rattle* Ekphrastic Challenge, June 2015, Editor's Choice; *Rattle* Ekphrastic Challenge, Artist's Choice, November 2016, Stephen A. DiBiase Poetry Prize, 2018; *Rattle* Ekphrastic Challenge, Editor's Choice, December, 2020. His twenty-four chapbooks include National Chapbook Contest winner *William Blake, Not Blessed Angel but Restless Man* (Red Ochre Press, 2014) and Turtle Island Editor's Choice Award *The Wire Fence Holding Back the World* (Flowstone Press, 2016). His twenty-two full-length books include *Ethereal Flowers* (Shanti Arts Publishing, 2023); National Ecological Award winner *Searching for What You Cannot See* (Hiraeth Press, 2013); *How to Be Silent* (FutureCycle Press, 2016); *Dylan Thomas and the Writer's Shed* (FutureCycle Press, 2017); *Three Ages of Women* (Deerbrook Editions, 2017); *Home Coming Celebration* (FutureCycle Press, 2019); 2019 Blue Light Award winner *The Temporary World*; *Unfolding of Love* (Wipf and Stock Publishers, 2020); and *Harvest Time* (Deerbrook Press, 2021).

SHANTI ARTS

NATURE ▪ ART ▪ SPIRIT

Please visit us online
to browse our entire book catalog,
including poetry collections and fiction,
books on travel, nature, healing, art,
photography, and more.

Also take a look at our highly regarded art
and literary journal, *Still Point Arts Quarterly*,
which may be downloaded for free.

www.shantiarts.com

www.ingramcontent.com/pod-product-compliance
Lightning Source LLC
LaVergne TN
LVHW060627110826
845147LV00015B/956

* 9 7 8 1 9 6 2 0 8 2 1 4 3 *